John Tinkler
Chattanooga
December 1, 1971

THE 26 *Letters*

Gothic

Rotunda

Italian cursive hands

Caroline

small letters

irish pointed   english pointed

irish semiuncial   english semiuncial

roman half uncial   Lombardic

ROMAN UNCIAL,   VERSALS

SQVARE CAP RVSTICS

ROMAN CAPITALS

The Family Tree of Our 26 Letters

The 26 Letters

REVISED EDITION

By Oscar Ogg

THOMAS Y. CROWELL COMPANY, New York

ESTABLISHED 1834

This book has been designed by the author and printed and bound by the Vail-Ballou Press, Inc. The body type is 14-point Linotype Caslon Old Face, chapter heads are 18-point A.T.F. Caslon 471. Paper is Warren's Sebago Antique.

Manufactured in the United States of America
L.C. Card 70-140646
ISBN 0-690-84115-9
1 2 3 4 5 6 7 8 9 10

Gratefully dedicated to my Mother who first taught me my 26 letters...

Preface to the Revised Edition

There are two compelling reasons for a new revised edition of this little book. First, since it was published more than twenty years ago, many mysteries of the past have been solved and some then-accepted dates and details have been amended through recent researches. It is unfair to leave them as mysteries and inaccuracies with the answers now at hand. Second, inventions and new developments which affect the use and design of the contemporary alphabet have come into being; these, too, belong in the story. They are discussed in a new chapter 10, "The Alphabet Today."

Finally, the book has gone through so many printings over the years that the type has become worn and the drawings ragged in places. To make for a more readable book we have taken pages from an early printing when the type was fresh and clean and converted them to offset lithography.

Table of Contents

Introduction

People have always wondered about the letters of the alphabet and where they came from. The Chinese tell how dragon-faced, four-eyed Ts'ang Chien invented the Chinese alphabet. He looked up and saw the patterns of

the stars. He looked down and saw the marks on the back of the turtle. He saw in his garden the footprints of birds.

From these patterns in nature, they say, Ts'ang Chien made the strange characters the Chinese use in writing.

Ts'ang Chien characters

Modern Chinese writing

Altars are found in all parts of China, on which any scrap of written paper was burned in his memory.

In Egypt, the weird-looking god Thoth, who had the head of a sacred bird, the ibis, was always pictured with the reed brush and the ink palette for writing in his hands.

The Egyptians believed that he invented all arts and sciences including their system of writing which they called "hieroglyphics"—sacred carvings.

In India, when the Hindu god Brahma decided to write down his teachings, there were no letters for him to use so he invented some. His patterns came mainly from the seams in the human skull. Brahma, they say, traced the first Hindu characters with his finger on leaves of gold.

A Greek legend says that Cadmus, a great national hero, brought the Greek letters—sixteen of them at least—from Phoenicia. Like many legends, this story has some foundation in truth, for we know that the Greeks did borrow most of their letters from the Phoenicians, who in turn probably got them from the Egyptians. Since many of our own capital letters came rather directly from the Greek alphabet, we see that there really is some reason for the rhyme:

Many thanks to old Cadmus, who made us his debtors, by inventing one day

THE CAPITAL LETTERS

Almost every people who have devised a system for writing—and there have been nearly two hundred separate alphabets that we know about—have had a legend or story to explain its origin. It is natural that they should, for alphabets develop gradually over centuries and their real origins are buried in the past.

About fifty different alphabets are in use today. Some are used for one language only, such as Greek; some are used for several languages, such as Arabic. Our own alphabet is the most widely used of any in the world. With it people write English, French, Spanish, Portuguese, Italian, Dutch, German, and Polish. Even the Turks are beginning to use it. With slight variations, it is the alphabet used by the Norwegians, the Swedes, and the Danes.

This great alphabet has had an amazingly long history. To understand its story, we could begin five thousand years ago in Egypt, with the hieroglyphics of the Nile dwellers, but to start at the *very* beginning we must go back more than 600,000 years.

Chapter 1

BEFORE HISTORY

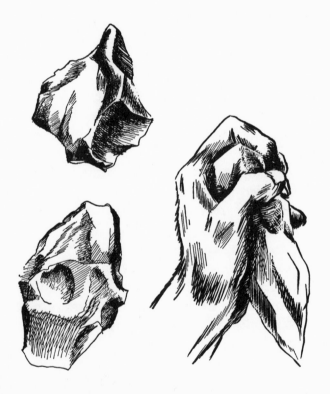

The very oldest relics of man's early predecessors are some broken pebbles whose edges were used to cut the hides of slain animals. They are about 1,500,000 years old and the creatures who made them were more like apes than men.

Gradually, as men evolved, so did tools. Broken pebbles were replaced by crudely chipped stones, which in turn developed slowly into hand axes, scrapers, and other tools. Some of the hand axes are more than 600,000 years old.

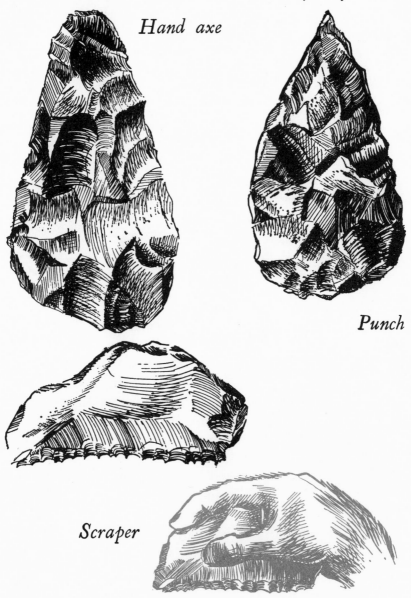

Hand axe

Punch

Scraper

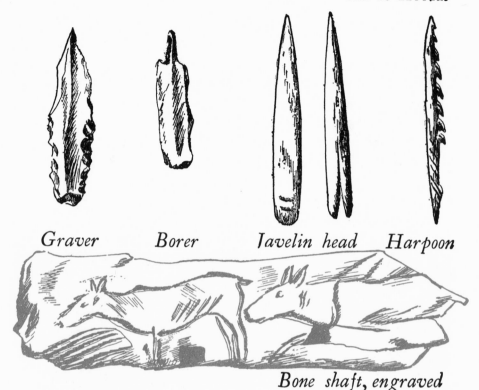

Graver   *Borer*   *Javelin head*   *Harpoon*

Bone shaft, engraved

Several hundred thousand more years crept by, and at last, about 35,000 years B.C. the first true men—human beings like ourselves—lived on the earth. They are called Reindeer men, for they hunted the reindeer in what is now northern Europe. Between 35,000 and 15,000 B.C. they developed well-made stone implements, such as gravers and borers, and javelin heads and fish spears of bone. It is with them that our story begins.

As far as we know, these were the first people to make pictures . . . bison and mammoths and saber-toothed tigers scratched on the walls of their caves. But don't imagine that this art sprang up overnight! Their own period of artistic development, more than twenty thousand years, was more than *ten times* as long as the whole Christian era.

We must remember that this first art, like all art, had a
reason for being. It was not "art for art's sake." The drawings, carvings, and paintings may have had religious significance, or may have served as fetishes of some kind—
hunting charms, perhaps. Or it may be that their use was
strictly practical. We do know that recently there was discovered in Spain a "memory helper" of reindeer horn left
by one of these ancient people. It was possibly a hunting
record or a war record, with a nick for every fallen enemy,
like the notches on the handles of western "six-guns"; or
it may have been a kind of calendar. No one knows . . . but
it did have some *practical* use.

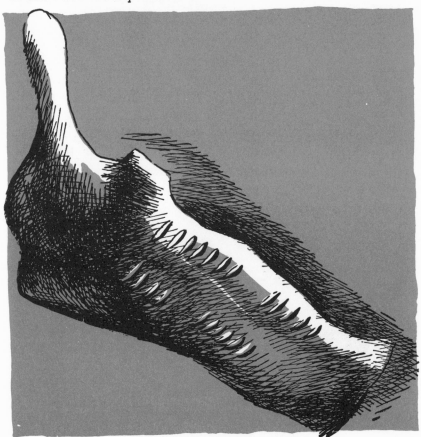

Other peoples had other kinds of graphic records. In Peru a thousand years ago (which seems no time at all, by comparison) the Incas used knotted cords, called *quipus*, for memory helpers. They, in fact, never did develop a system of writing and they depended entirely on these memory helpers for tax records, historical records, and even for transmitting messages.

A great-grandchild of the quipus exists right now, in the present . . . the string you tie around your finger to remind you of some duty.

When the Reindeer men first made pictures, they simply scratched them upon bits of bone . . . like engravings.

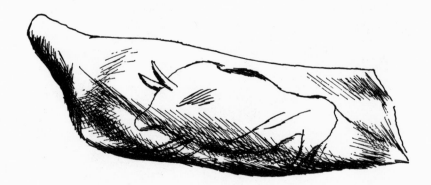

As time went on, they cut them deeper and deeper into the surface . . . like bas relief.

Finally the designs were fully carved "in the round," and real sculpture was created.

Although twenty thousand or more years old, this carved
reindeer-horn spear thrower is far from crude.

With these most primitive pieces of art as a background, let us turn to the earliest drawings.

One summer afternoon, some fifty years ago, a scientist who gathered and studied the relics of bygone ages to learn how ancient people lived, was searching a cave at Altamira, near the town of Santillana in northern Spain. First he collected the weapons of stone and flint, the bones, pots, and tools which he found on the floor of the cave. Then he began to dig down, layer by layer, through the relics left by preceding families.

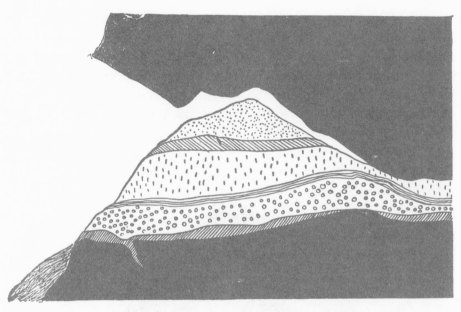

Natural rock of the cave | 75,000 years ago | 50,000 years ago | 40,000 years ago | 25,000 years ago | 20,000 years ago | 10,000 years ago

These ancient peoples were apparently a slovenly lot and left everything lying about. When they departed suddenly for war or for the hunt, or when they moved to another cave, they left all their goods behind them and made new stone axes and spears and utensils for their new home. And when other families occupied the cave hundreds or even thousands of years later, the dust of ages and the crumbling walls or roof of the cave had covered over the relics of the earlier tenants, and they, not bothering with housecleaning, made their home on top of these. So the archeologist, digging through these remains, is able to determine how cave dwellers lived at different times back through the ages.

By the sputtering light of his lamp far back in the dark
cave, our scientist, the Marquis de Sautuola, was digging
away while his little five-year-old daughter, who had come
with him that day, sat quietly and watched him. Finally

she grew tired of looking at the stone axes and bone spears which he uncovered with his spade; and, taking a candle to light her way, she wandered farther back into the dust-covered, inky-dark tunnel which led uphill and down, back into the hillside.

Suddenly she stopped. There before her, awesome in the flickering light, was a shaggy bison.

As she stood staring, she realized that she was not looking at a live animal but at a painting. It had appeared so lifelike on the wall in the dim light that it had seemed ready to spring down upon her from the ledge of rock.

As soon as she could gather her wits about her, she turned and ran for her father. "*Toros! Toros!*" (Bulls! Bulls!") she shouted. The marquis thought at first that she was making up a story about what she had imagined in the dark cave. But when he realized she was deadly earnest, he took up his lantern and followed her.

He too was awed by the splendid drawing and thought it must be the work of some modern prankster. No footprints were in evidence anywhere in the thick dust, however, except his own and those of the little girl.

Together they went deeper into the cave and found other drawings. The little girl led the way and the marquis followed, stooping, for the ceiling was very low. Thus were discovered the now famous Altamira wall paintings which scientists agree are the work of Reindeer men, whose home was the cave itself.

It was only a few years later that two boys of twelve and fourteen, playing in a cave on the banks of the Dordogne River in France, discovered other drawings and paintings like those at Altamira.

Since then, more have been unearthed at Combarelles and Font-de-Gaume and other caves.

It is not likely that any of these marvelous cave paintings were made just for show. Most of them are placed deep in the farthest corners where they can hardly be seen at all. In the cave at Font-de-Gaume in France there are twenty-five different drawings and not one of them is illumined by the daylight that comes in the entrance.

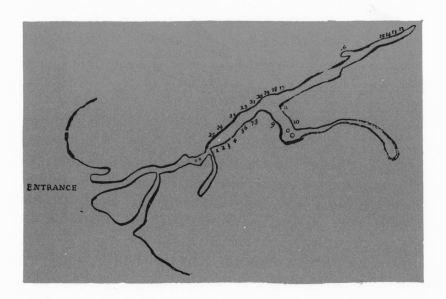

Drawings were made by the primitive artists on the
natural rock of the cave walls and ceilings with charcoal,
some kind of coloring material applied with a skin pad, and
a few wood or bone tools. The veining of the rock often
suggested the size and shape of the drawings, as of this
bison in which the artist has followed the bulge of the rock
in drawing the hump.

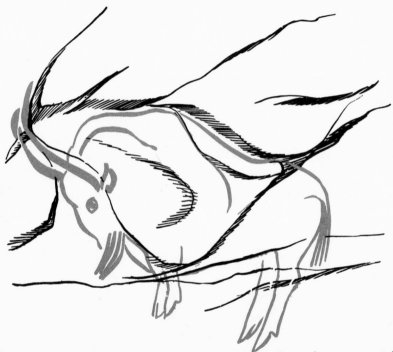

We can see from these fragments, taken from several
places in Europe, that the first drawings on the cave walls
were of animals—usually bison and mammoths. Sometimes
there is a whole beast, sometimes only the head. Often the
drawings are sketchy and incomplete, but some of them
are wonderfully distinct and detailed.

The very earliest drawings show the animals just standing. They were merely portraits of the bison and mam-

moths and deer and tigers which the cave man hunted. No attempt was made to get action into the pictures. The artist seemed satisfied to say with his painting, "This is a deer," or "This is a bison."

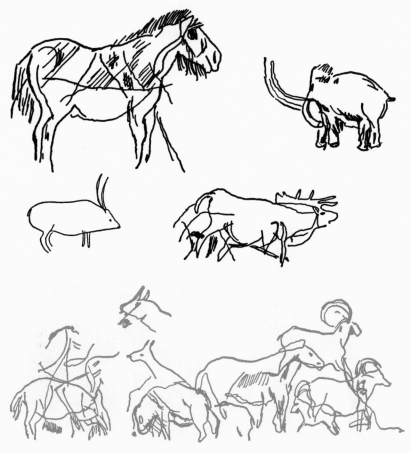

A long step toward picture-stories was taken when the painter showed the animals in action—showed them running, fighting, eating, dying.

Today with our action photographs and movies, our comic strips and illustrations, the putting of action into pictures seems a small thing. It was, however, a tremendously important development when the cave artists began to make pictures tell stories.

Here are a galloping horse, a running bison, two deer fighting. These drawings have become story-pictures. The artist had decided that he wanted to say more; he wanted to tell about two deer he had seen fighting. The picture would recall to those who had seen a reindeer fight what the artist had in mind when he drew. The artist was communicating, telling a *picture-story*.

It is important to realize that this growth from just drawings to story-drawings took place everywhere at approximately the same period. Long before traveling great distances, or visiting other tribes was possible, artists in widely separated sections of the world were developing at about the same rate—without any outside influences.

The drawings on these pages are from Spain and France and southern Europe, yet all of them are similar in spirit.

In the earliest drawings the subjects seem always to have been animals. We seldom see human beings in the scenes. Later, however, a few pictures began to be made which included people.

Like the first pictures of animals, they showed no action. They were just people standing, or sitting, or lying down. Such a drawing said little more than, "This is a man."

Again, as with the early animal pictures, the first drawings of human beings were not always complete. Sometimes there was only a face or a head, but occasionally there was a whole figure represented, as the woman from southern Europe and the four little people from Africa.

At last the pictures of people began to show action too. Men and women were drawn running, shooting arrows, going on trips, sleeping, hunting, eating. Now they also became part of a picture-story.

Here is a hunting party in the field. The picture tells a story familiar to every Stone Age man. This tiny bit of the complete hunting trip serves to recount fully a small part of the whole story and to suggest the rest. It is in drawings such as this that we find the first beginnings of real writing. The picture, though incomplete for us, tells a complete story to those familiar with the subject.

Women in ceremonial hunt dance   Sighting the quarry

Leaving for the hunt

This is the way an artist might have "written" a whole
story of a hunting trip. We see here all the different ele-

The kill

Surrounding the quarry

The return home

ments of a great hunt, from the ceremony before the hunters leave to the return with the dead animals.

There is this trouble with a picture-story, however:
You have to know something about the story already or
the picture cannot convey to you what the artist had in
mind. For example, this early Egyptian wall carving shows
action, as do the prehistoric hunting scenes. To us it seems
to portray two ancient cowboys in pursuit of a steer. To an
Egyptian, however, it showed the catching of a sacred bull
for sacrifice. This one picture-story could bring to his mind
a complete ceremony, an important part of his religion;
he *already knew* what the artist was trying to tell about.

The first great improvement in telling a picture-story
came with the use of a *series* of related pictures, which
showed an action step by step. These nine scenes, for example, depict the progress of a wrestling match.

Then came another step. In telling picture-stories, "authors" gradually came to use picture *symbols* instead of lifelike pictures of the objects they represented. The *picture* of a man, for instance, might change according to the whim of the artist, but the *symbol* would not change, unless the meaning changed. So at this point real picture-words were used. We are drawing closer to the alphabet.

These four figures show how a symbol, a simplified basic drawing, gradually replaced a picture for the word "man."

The American Indians' use of pictures to convey messages is well known. This is the way it was done. Each little picture represented an idea or a thing. Together they told a story . . . if you guessed and filled in where necessary. Here is a very famous one:

Home—(I) leave—(to go on a journey in a) canoe— (to be gone for) ten (days).—(I arrive on an) island (on which live) two families—(and there I meet a) friend.— We go together in my canoe—to (another) island— (where) we hunt with bows and arrows.—(We kill a) sea lion.—(We start our) return (journey—and) my friend returns in the canoe with me.—(After) ten (days— I arrive) home.

This is true *picture writing*, the forerunner of alphabetic writing. However, it cannot yet be called a standard system of writing because the pictures might be drawn quite differently by another writer. The same story might not be diagramed in the same way twice . . . and the story, also, might be read by different people to mean different things.

Many nations developed picture-writing for themselves.
These examples are from Scandinavia, Sweden, North
Europe, America, Egypt, and China.

By the time picture-writing advanced to this stage, the artist discovered that he could give character to his symbols by adding characteristic features, as in these Indian symbols for "man": a spear for a hunter, a cane for an old man, and many others.

Man   Hunter   Chief   Friend

Long-legged man   Cripple   Old man

Of course in time thing-pictures came to be used for all the common physical things.

And now a new feature appeared in the use of pictures for story telling . . . a feature which later was to lead to drawing *ideas* as well as *things*. For instance, one could say "ten warriors" by drawing a warrior picture with ten marks under it. One could write with symbols *canoe, sun, earth, one week, water, mountains, three afternoons, home, ten cows,* and *hunter*. Thus, not only had the pictures themselves become symbols but their use likewise had outgrown simple thing-pictures. The artist no longer needed ten cow symbols to say "ten cows," he drew *one* cow and put ten marks below it: ten cows!

Some of these pictures represent things which you can
see. The picture of the sun is one of these. Others represent
things which you cannot see. The sun with seven marks
(meaning *week*) is one of these.

But even these simplified thing-pictures, in their new
usage, had a serious disadvantage: they could not say
enough. It was easy to make a drawing of a man—or a
symbol for man—stand for the word *man*. The same was
true with *bison*, or *sun*, or *canoe*, or *week*. But how would
you draw a picture of *happiness?* or *sorrow? love? hate?*
Idea-pictures were needed as well as thing-pictures.

The first idea-signs were probably made through the
joining together of two or more thing-signs. For example,
early writers had already simplified their drawing for
water until they had arrived at a little wavy-line symbol.
The sign for *mouth* had likewise become a very simple
picture of two lips. Add *water* to *mouth* and you have
drink. Two *thing-pictures* may be combined to produce
an *idea-picture*.

In the same way *eye* plus *water* equals *weep*. *Mouth* plus
bread equals *eat*. *Woman* plus *son* equals *love*.

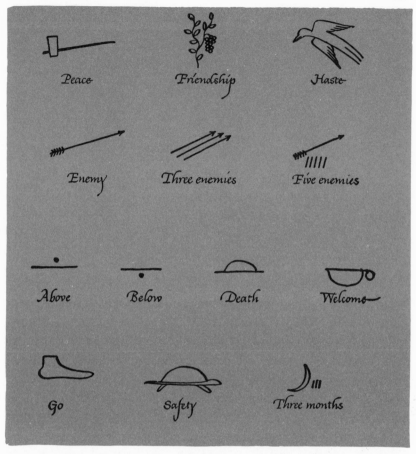

Idea-pictures came to be made in another way: a picture of an object would gradually come to represent some idea connected with it, rather than the thing itself. For example, the peace pipe was smoked at Indian pow-wows as a symbol of peace. What could be more natural than for the symbol of the pipe to have the meaning of *peace?*

A famous example from Crete, a signet ring, is reported to have had carved upon it a sailing ship with a moon on either side of the mast. This was an idea-picture used as a trademark or signature. It showed that whatever property

was marked with this seal belonged to the owner of the ring. It is probable that all who knew the owner of the seal considered his idea-signature a very logical one indeed for he is believed to have been a seaman famous because he dared to make trips lasting as long as two moons!

It is clear that more complete stories became possible with these idea-pictures, but it is a mistake to suppose that idea-pictures were suddenly used *instead of* thing-pictures. Both were used, and they continued to be used side-by-side for centuries.

As time went on, the system became more and more complicated, but it never overcame this disadvantage: one could never be sure he had read the message right. For instance, Herodotus, the Greek historian, tells how such a misunderstanding brought disaster to an overconfident Persian general.

When Darius, in 512 B.C., invaded the land of the Scythians, a herald came to him with a message from the enemy. It was an idea-picture. Darius was too proud to admit to the enemy herald that he could not read the message. He studied it in secret the whole night through.

Next morning he called his generals together and proclaimed to them that he had found the meaning of the pictures. "Thus," he said, "the enemy writes: 'O Persians, we surrender our land and our water [the mouse and the

frog]. We fly [the bird] from the might of your legions.
We are ready to turn over to you all of our arms [the
arrows].' Behold, O Persian generals, the cowardly Scythians want to surrender to us even before they have felt
the might of our swords."

That night the Scythians made an attack on the Persian
camp—much to the surprise of the Persian invaders who
believed the Scythian army had fled.

Darius discovered from a Scythian commander after the
battle that the message had really meant: "O Persians,
unless you can turn yourselves into birds and fly through
the air, or become as field mice and burrow under the
ground, or be as frogs and take refuge in the swamps, you
shall never escape to return to your native land but will die
by our arrows."

Up to this point, writing symbols had made their meanings clear by what they looked like. A thing-picture of a
man looked like a man; an idea-picture for *peace* looked
like a peace pipe.

There is another way of writing words. That is to use
symbols that will make the *sound* of the spoken word clear.
That is the system we use. We put together the twenty-six
letters in all sorts of combinations to reproduce the sounds
that we make when talking. What we have is sound-pictures, instead of thing-pictures or idea-pictures.

No matter how we write *man*, whether in small letters
or large, it never looks like a man, but when we read or
pronounce the word, then the word *man* comes out.

The time finally came when the ancients put into writing the sounds of their spoken words. But at first it was not
with letters.

This is how it came about: you have often solved puz-
zles that used pictures instead of words—where you had
to make out the answer from little pictures. For instance,
the word *be* would be shown as a picture of a bee, and the

word *I* as a picture of an eye. You might have a series of pictures like this:

As mere pictures they have no connection, but when you say the words out loud you have a perfectly good sentence:

I CAN SAW WOOD

It would be almost impossible to write everything this way, but there are many pairs of words that have the same sounds. They can be used as puns, like *made* and *maid*, *be* and *bee*, *ball* and *bawl*. The Egyptians used such puns in pictures for their writing.

For instance, it happened that in ancient Egyptian the word for *hear* sounded the same as the one for *paint the eyes*. So sometimes in Egyptian writing a picture of an ear instead of being read *ear* or *hear* was read *paint the eyes* because the word sound meant both.

To make picture signs of things was easy. To make picture signs of ideas was harder. To make picture signs for some words and ideas was impossible. For instance, how would you draw a picture of the meaning of a word like *in* or *approach?*

As we know, the Egyptians got around it again in the same way. Suppose you wanted to draw—not write—*in*. You could draw a *picture* of an *inn* and the reader would probably guess what you meant.

Well, the Egyptians (and the Chinese too) did exactly
the same thing. Their word for *in* was *khen*. Their word
for *approach* was *kheny*. *Khen* also meant *hide* or *skin*. That
was easy to draw like this:

The result? They used a picture of a hide for *skin* (khen),
approach (kheny) and *in* (khen).

Of course to see how this worked you have to know a
little of the Egyptian vocabulary. Here is an example in
our own language. Suppose you wanted to draw a picture
of the word *conceal*. That would be hard to do, but you
could draw a picture of a hide; *to hide* means to conceal.

Not only words but syllables can be represented that
way. The word *hide*, which we have just been talking
about, could be the first syllable of hyd-ro, as in *hydro-
plane*. You could make a picture of a hide stand for the first
syllable, and a man rowing for the second.

This is how the word *penmanship* would look if we used picture puns:

The Egyptians did this, too. Their word for *turquoise* was *khesteb*. *Khes* meant *stop* and *teb* meant *pig*. It was an easy matter to supply an idea-picture for *khes* and a thing-picture *teb*. The combined pictures, shown here as they

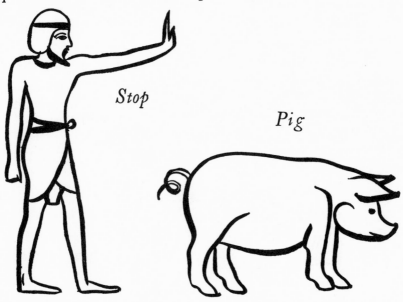

Stop

Pig

might have been drawn (but probably weren't!) make a
perfectly good sound-picture for *khesteb*.

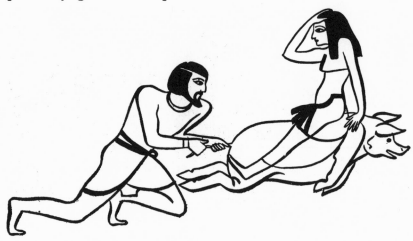

If, on the other hand, the two were taken together as
mere thing-pictures the meaning would certainly be quite
different. It would be simply, "Man stops pig."

Finally there is the possibility of using pictures not for
whole words, not for syllable sounds, but for letters. That,
of course, is our system.

The Egyptians, too, used a system of letters. For them
a picture of an eagle meant *a*; a picture of a leg meant *b*;
a picture of a hand meant *d*. In fact they used all at the same
time: thing-pictures, idea-pictures, and sound-pictures.

Thing-picture

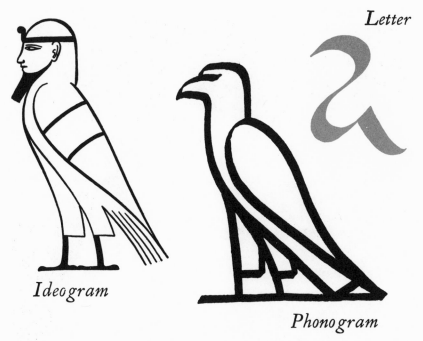

Letter

Ideogram

Phonogram

Take the eagle, for instance. First it was a thing-picture drawn to look like an eagle and meaning *eagle*. Then it received a human face and became an idea-picture meaning *soul*. But also it was used, still looking like an eagle, to represent the letter *a*. Finally in another type of Egyptian writing (hieratic) it came to look like a letter, and no longer like a picture.

It is with the Egyptians that the alphabet really begins, but they never did actually develop one for themselves because they did not use letters *exclusively*. Their writing went through the five main steps we have seen pictures take: (1) thing-pictures; (2) idea-pictures; (3) word-sound pictures; (4) syllable-sound pictures and (5) letter-sound pictures—and retained a little of them all, plus an explanatory symbol or two for each word. The true alphabet uses only letter-sound pictures.

Chapter 2

THE EGYPTIANS

A hundred and fifty years ago Napoleon set out to conquer the world. Among other places, he sent his legions into Egypt. His plans, like those of other selfish, ambitious rulers, ended in failure. However, at least one good thing came out of his ill-fated expedition: the key to Egyptian hieroglyphics. And that was pure accident.

For centuries these picture writings of ancient Egypt, great quantities of them, had kept their secrets as silently as the Sphinx itself. They are to be found almost every-

where throughout the Nile Valley—on the remains of
temples that overlook the river, painted with reed brushes

on the interiors of subterranean tombs whose thick stone walls were covered over for thousands of years by the hot sands of the desert. They appear in both public and private ruins, on stone, wood, papyrus. But, until after Napoleon had come to Egypt, no modern man had ever been able to decipher or interpret them.

One August day in 1799 the accident happened. A certain Lieutenant Boussard, a young officer in Napoleon's engineers, was strolling about the village of Rosetta near the mouth of the Nile. He noticed a slab of rock about four feet long that was sticking out of the sandy earth. It

was basalt, a black stone. The rock attracted his curiosity.
He noticed that it was covered with odd characters that he
could not read, and he reported his find to his superior,
General Menou. Menou realized that the stone was a valuable thing and immediately had it taken to his home. However, Napoleon heard of the discovery and ordered that it
be deposited in Cairo for study. Then he had men come
down from Paris to make rubbings for further study.

When Napoleon was finally defeated, the British,
having heard of this remarkable curio, put a special clause
in the treaty of capitulation, to gain possession of it. Meanwhile Menou had taken the stone back home again and
insisted that it was his personal possession. Needless to say,
the British obliged him to surrender the relic, and the
much-traveled, much-disputed stone was shipped to England, where it is now on view in the British Museum.

What were these characters that provoked so much
curiosity and made everyone want to gain possession of the
Rosetta stone itself? They were of three kinds: at the top,
Egyptian hieroglyphics (the writing for monumental
works); in the middle, demotic (the writing of ordinary
life); at the bottom, Greek. The contents of the inscription, which had been cut in 196 B.C., were not particularly
important. What *was* important was that the same thing
had been written in three ways, and that one of these was
Greek, which could be read with ease. Of course they were
not sure at first that this was the case, but they *hoped* so,
and the more they studied the surer they became.

One might imagine that after this decision was made,
translation would be easy; but, when you consider that
no one knew whether the signs were words or letters or
symbols, you will realize what a task it was. Decoding the
Rosetta stone turned out to be a tremendously difficult job.
The work was handed on from one scholar to another for
forty years. Of these scholars there was one—Jean Fran-

çois Champollion—who spent his whole career in the work and who finally found the key.

For twenty years after the discovery of the stone little real progress was made. Then an Englishman, Dr. Thomas Young, proved that at least some of the characters were letters of a sort, not just pictures. He even worked out a translation of several groups. He is usually credited with establishing the sound values of six of the hieroglyphs.

That was the beginning. Then came the work of the great Frenchman Champollion, aided by his son.

An important feature of the Rosetta stone is half a dozen ovals with characters inside. Champollion of course noticed these at once, and he guessed that several of them contained the name *Ptolemy*, which appeared plainly enough in the Greek below.

Now Champollion recalled an obelisk he had seen on the island of Philae in the Nile. It, too, displayed Greek inscriptions at the base, hieroglyphs above. It, too, had these undeciphered ovals, or cartouches, and the names *Ptolemy* and *Cleopatra* in Greek.

This is where Champollion picked up his first clue. He saw how similar were the ovals which he guessed contained *Ptolemy*— the ones on the obelisk and the ones on the Rosetta stone. He

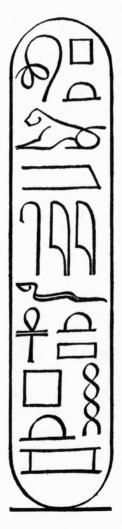

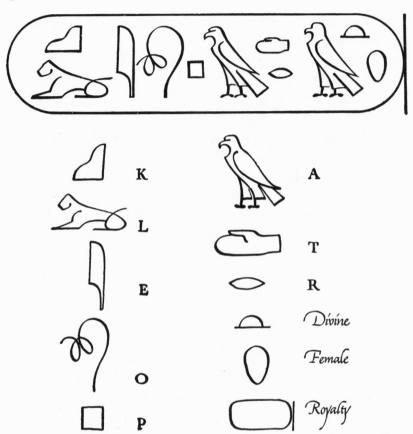

knew then that he was right, and that this was an important step. For the first time in centuries these strange Egyptian pictures were giving up their secret.

Later he identified the Cleopatra ovals on both stones. This gave him more material to work with. He now had a key, though a small one.

Fortunately both Ptolemy and Cleopatra contain some of the same characters—the character for *L*, for instance. Here was another clue. Comparing these two words in the two different places, Champollion found the values of thirteen characters. He used other inscriptions and monuments. Next he deciphered *Alexander* which supplied three more signs. Step by step he went through all the proper names he could find, adding to his supply of known characters with each. At last, he could read whole sentences. And then before his work was completely finished, he died. But Champollion had found the key. After him his son, and after his son Rosellini, de Rougé, and others used that key to unlock the written language of this ancient people.

Here, much enlarged, is the Cleopatra oval and the key used by the French scholar in translating the hieroglyph. The knee, which looks like a piece of pie, stands for *K*; the lion for *L*; next the leaf for *I* (or our *E*); the knotted cord for *O*; the shutter (the square) for *P*; the eagle for *A*; the hand for *D* or *T*; the mouth for *R*; again the eagle for *A*. Then *Kleopatra*.

But there are still two symbols beyond the second eagle, and the oval itself, to consider. These, it turns out, are not letters but idea-pictures. They stand for words. Again the key yields *divine*, *female*, *royalty* or *divine queen*. So the hieroglyph adds up to *Cleopatra, Divine Queen*.

Notice that Cleopatra is spelled out, phonetically, and idea-pictures are used for *Divine Queen*. If the Egyptians had also spelled out *Divine* and *Queen*, they would have been using a true alphabet straight through—but they never did. They continued to use a mixture of systems.

Occasionally, even today, we too use a mixture of two systems. You have seen road signs like this:

Just as in Egyptian five thousand years ago, it is both spelled out and pictured.

Egyptian history, more than twice as long as the history of Christian civilization, stretches back to fifty centuries before Christ. When the tomb of the first true Egyptian king was discovered, characters were found that date back some five thousand years!

In the earlier stages, hieroglyphics were used only by the priests (in fact *hieroglyphic* means priest-writing) and for monumental inscriptions which were usually carved or painted. Later they were both written and painted, and used by the common people as well.

Altogether more than three thousand of the odd-looking characters have been found, but only about three hundred were commonly used.

When we look at the characters in a hieroglyphic inscription, we see a great many figures of animals and birds —a lioness, an owl, an eagle, a serpent—and sometimes there are curious combinations of birds or animals with human features—a man with a bird's head, or a lion with a human head like that of the great Sphinx. Animals were closely associated with the Egyptian religion, and to the Egyptians their religion meant much.

We may suppose that once, in the beginning, various animals had been used as the symbols of different tribes. Just as Boy Scout patrols today are called the "Beaver" or the "Eagle," so many of the early Egyptian tribes had animal mascots which were supposed to bring them good luck. In time the mascot became more and more important to the members of the tribe and gradually it came to be thought of as having qualities above those of mere human beings. The eagle, for instance, became the symbol of the soul after death. As the Egyptian religion developed over a period of centuries, animals came to be associated with certain gods. When a picture of a god was made, he was shown as having some part of the mascot about him. At

Ra   Sekhet

times he was given the mascot's head; at times the wings, the fur, or feathers; and sometimes the whole body.

It is not surprising then that the hieroglyphic writing should use many animal and bird symbols. But there were other symbols also. Some of them resembled common objects, and others are apparently so much simplified from earlier drawings that there is only slight resemblance.

Some pictures kept on being used to represent the objects they resembled. Others came to be used as letters.

You will recognize here the eagle for *A* and the lion for *L*. Although most of these pictures are more elaborate than our own letters, they served very well. In some cases they are quite simple. The hieroglyph for *R*, as an example, is even simpler than our own letter.

Anyone would naturally expect that Egyptian writing would have abandoned pictures-for-things and pictures-for-ideas when it got to the point where it could spell out words with perfectly good letter signs.

Actually it did no such thing. Hieroglyphs were used as letters even in the earliest known Egyptian writings. The

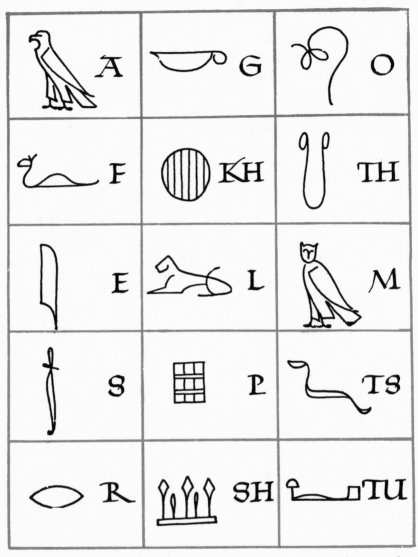

inscription of King Menes, over 5,000 years old, contains them. Indeed, as time went on, more and more of the thing-pictures and idea-pictures were used.

This desire to retain the old, established pictures is one of the interesting characteristics of the Egyptian people. They held their ancestors in great respect, they revered all ancient things, and their love of the past is most clearly shown in their writing system.

Of course this reverence for established orders is not unique with the Egyptians. All human beings tend to keep to the old ways even while they are adding the new.

The Egyptians did, however, as their ancestors before them and their offspring since, *change* and *add to* the meanings of many of the pictures they retained.

At one stage the system of hieroglyphics contained four hundred different symbols, and was very complicated. It is no wonder that there were so many—five different types of hieroglyphics were all in use at the same time.

First, there were pictures of things, which we have been calling thing-pictures.

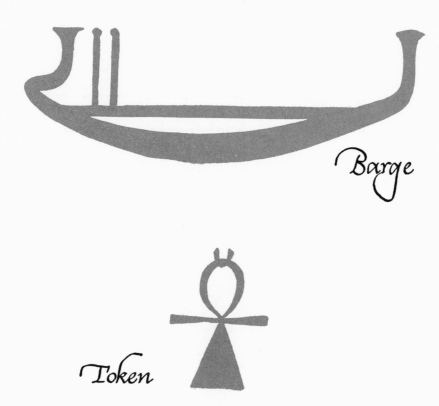

Barge

Token

Second, there were idea-pictures developed from the original thing-pictures. For instance, the picture of a leg, which first meant *leg*, became *run* and finally *fleet*.

The picture of a hand had at first merely meant *hand*, then *work*, then finally *power*.

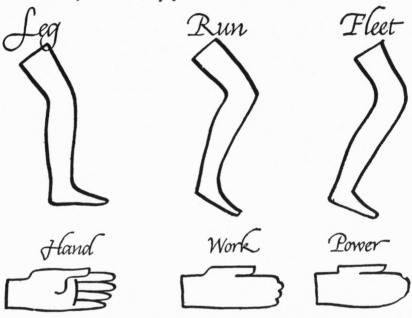

The more they used the idea-picture system, the more it was developed. The drawing for an eagle, a bird which was much admired and frequently used as a decoration, was stretched to mean *soul*. A human head was supplied to show that in such cases *eagle* was no longer meant.

They employed pictures for ideas increasingly, but they continued the use of thing-pictures, too.

Finally came the most important step of all . . . they began to use sound-pictures (the third type of hiero-glyphic). For instance, the wavy line for *water* (in Egyptian, *nu*) came to mean simply the sound of *N*. The result was a letter just as good as our *N*, and very much like it.

The sign for *mouth* (in Egyptian, *ro*) came to stand for the sound of *R*.

In this way some of their thing- and idea-pictures gradually turned into sound-pictures, and some of those sound-pictures into what we would call syllables and letters. These syllables and letters were the fourth and fifth types of hieroglyphics.

There were then, at this point, five divisions in the system of writing:

(1) Thing-pictures (as the picture of a token for the word *token*).

(2) Idea-pictures (as the picture of a sinking sun for the word *death*).

(3) Sound-pictures for whole words (as the picture of a hide for *approach*).

(4) Other pictures for syllables (as the whip for *mes*).

(5) Still others for letter sounds (as the mouth for *R*).

It was this step to pictures of letters that made the whole system workable. Many sound-pictures of words and many sound-pictures of syllables were eventually eliminated.

Even the sound pictures of letters were reduced in number, for previously there had been as many as thirty signs for the sound of *A*.

The whole number of letter-sound-pictures was cut down to forty-five, and finally to twenty-five.

There was still one step between the Egyptians' hieroglyphics and a true alphabet like our own, which was never taken. The Nile dwellers never gave up their symbols for whole words and their pictures for ideas.

Of the letter sounds, the Egyptians had a first-string "alphabet" of twenty-three. With this plus a kind of second-string alphabet they could spell out all of their words more or less as we spell ours.

They were not content, however, to use this system of letters alone. As we have just said, they kept using the thing-pictures and idea-pictures, too. They hitched them on afterwards by way of explanation. The reason for this practice was probably that so many of their words had many meanings. *Ab* could mean twenty different things; *ha* forty!

Take *sef* for instance. When it meant *yesterday*, a picture of the sun was drawn next to the word; when it meant *baby* it was followed by a picture of a child.

The word *ab* was spelled with only two letters, of course, but when it meant "thirst" the Egyptians thought it necessary to hitch on *three* pictures as explanation: a dog jumping up, wavy lines for water, a man pointing to his mouth.

Another thing which made these explanatory pictures necessary was that the Egyptians never got around to spelling anything the same way every time. In the fourteenth line of the Rosetta stone the word *writing* occurs four times. The first time it is spelled out, then explained by a picture of a man writing. The second and third times it is pictured by a reed and an ink bottle. In the fourth instance it is spelled out again, and this time in another way!

The decorative "explaining signs" were used increasingly. This of course meant that the writing became increasingly complicated. If only the letter signs had been retained and the accompanying pictures discarded entirely, it would have been the Egyptians, rather than a later people, who were responsible for the first true alphabet.

Besides their enormous contribution to the beginnings of the alphabet, the Egyptians also invented an excellent material on which to write —papyrus. This was a paper-like material that was used for books, letters, documents, or any other writing, and it was infinitely cheaper and more plentiful than the other early writing stock, animal skin.

The papyrus plant is a kind of giant swamp grass that grows in river mud. It sometimes grows to a height of ten feet and its roots are often as thick as a man's arm. The Egyptians probably transplanted it from what is now Ethiopia and raised it in the Nile delta. Ropes, mats, clothing, even the sails of boats were made from it, and the stalk could be cooked and eaten as well!

The making of paper from papyrus for writing purposes is not an easy process. The pith has to be removed from the inside of the stalk. It is then cut into strips as thin and wide as possible. These strips are placed in rows very close together. They are covered with paste made of flour and boiling water and then overlaid with a layer of strips running the opposite way. The two layers of pulp are beaten gently until a thin sheet is obtained; this is dried in the sun, and finally polished by burnishing with an agate or a smooth shell.

Egyptian papyrus became the most generally used writing material of the ancient world. Alexandria grew to be the center of the papyrus industry and her papyrus was exported in huge quantities. Many of the great manuscripts of early Greek and Roman literature were written upon it.

We have seen that hieroglyphics were at first inscribed upon basalt, granite and sandstone, or carved into wood and plaster. But when the Egyptians developed papyrus they produced something which could be written upon with brush or pen. It could be made in any size or weight, and papyri have been found that are one hundred and forty feet long. Fortunately it was more durable than much of our paper. The oldest known piece goes back three thousand years B.C.

Materials, of course, are the most important influence in the development of implements. The chisel was needed for inscription in stone, the gouge or graver for inscription on wood. For writing on paper a new tool was called for. The

Egyptians found the tool to write with as well as the paper to write on. They took a reed, frayed the end a bit to make a sort of brush, dipped it in a liquid that was like our ink, and wrote with it.

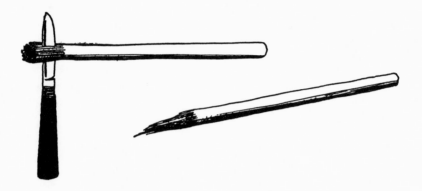

Later the reed was shaped and split at the point very much like our present-day pen. Actually such a pen, made

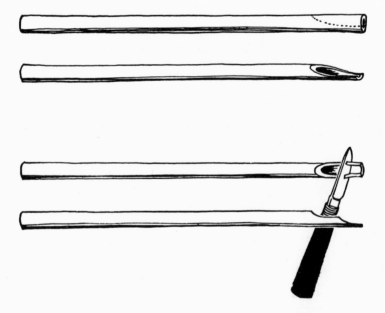

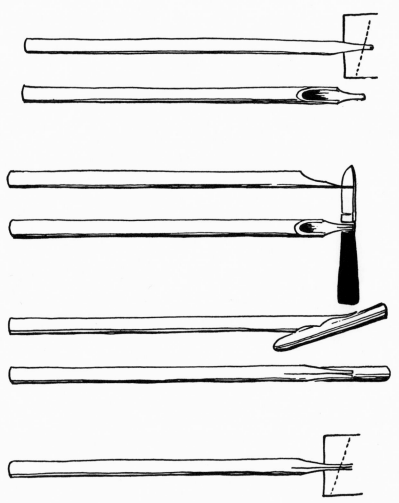

from a reed or a quill, is far superior to a steel pen for fine
writing. It is softer and more pliable; and, even to this day,
fine writing is almost always done with a reed or a quill
pen, prepared almost exactly as the Egyptians used to do.

Writing with a pen on papyrus instead of with a brush
or a carving tool on a stone was bound to make a difference

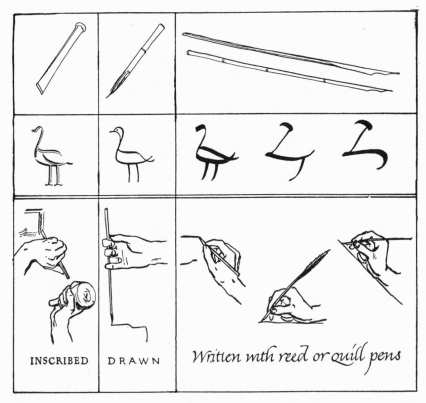

INSCRIBED   DRAWN   *Written with reed or quill pens*

in the style of writing. The use of the reed pen brought about a simplified form of the earlier picture letters. This and the need for more rapid writing than was possible with the handsome but cumbersome hieroglyphs brought about, around 3500 B.C., a new system of symbols based on the hieroglyphs. The new writing was called *hieratic*, again meaning "of the priests," for it was used at first only to record sacred literature.

Later, of course, because of its simplicity and speed, it was used for all kinds of government documents, private memoranda and nearly all writing except the most monumental records.

It is easy to see how much more quickly and easily one could write with such characters, each requiring only one

Hieroglyphic	Changing		Hieratic

or two strokes of the pen. In the beginning hieratics were actually nothing more than "speeded-up" forms of the hieroglyphs themselves. They went through many stages of change and development, however, and in the end they were to hieroglyphics almost what our "handwriting" is to our formal type designs.

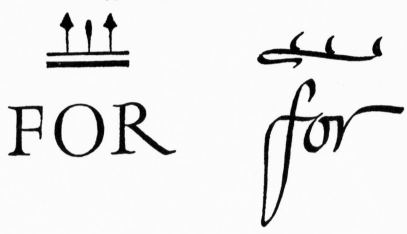

The most famous hieratic manuscript is called *The Book of the Dead*. Written on papyrus with a reed pen, it was composed no one knows how long ago; the earliest remaining copies are over five thousand years old. It deals mainly

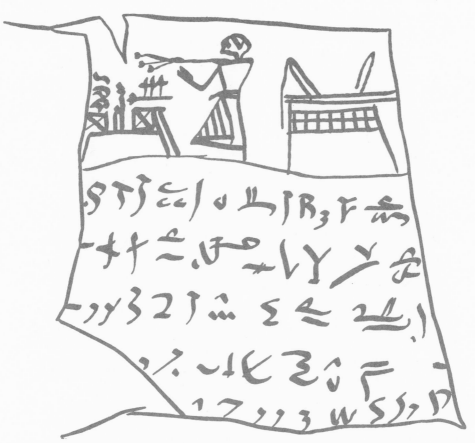

with the funeral ritual. A great part of the book, however, tells about the Ka, or soul, and how it makes its trip from the tomb to the next world, going through many adventures before it settles down to a happy life in the eternal. It will be seen from the illustration that though the book itself was written in hieratic script, hieroglyphics were used for the decorative parts of the manuscript. During all the years that the hieratic writing was in use, the Egyptians clung to their fine old picture writing, so rich in associations and legends, and employed it in all "fine writing" in books, on buildings and monuments and tombs.

The Egyptians also developed a third style of writing even simpler and easier to write. It is the form we call *demotic* (from the Greek word *demos* meaning "the

people"). We may remember that it was the style of writing used in the middle inscription on the famous Rosetta stone. The demotic letters were beautiful, legible, could be made rapidly and were true "pen forms." This was the writing used in trade and commerce.

Certainly it was getting very close to a true alphabet.

Since the Egyptians did not arrive at a true alphabet, who were the first to have one? The credit for making that last step toward a writing system without any pictures or reminder-symbols is generally given to the Phoenicians.

Chapter 3

THE PHOENICIANS

The Phoenicians were traders, hard and keen. They left no literature, no books and few inscriptions. They needed the alphabet for business, for lists of goods, inventories and accounting records. It is just because their alphabet did serve this purpose, that they stripped away all the pictures and produced a very much simplified system.

Phoenicia was the coastal portion of the country which we now call Syria. It was a barren, rocky land, and it is no wonder that the inhabitants found the sea more friendly. They called themselves Canaanites and they did, in fact, belong to the Canaanite peoples as the Biblical term is used. The Greeks gave them the name Phoenicians, meaning "blood-red," probably because of the brilliant crimson clothes worn by their sailors.

It is hard to read their history without feeling some pity for them, in spite of their avarice and greed. They started out by being a subject people of the Egyptians. Then between 1200 B.C. and 876 B.C. they had a brief period of independence. (Much longer than our country has been independent, however!) After that they were conquered in turn by the Assyrians, Babylonians, Persians, and Macedonians. The last must have been the worst. At one time Alexander decided to make an example of Tyre as Hitler

did of Lidice. Eight thousand Tyrians were put to the
sword and thirty thousand sold as slaves. Now the harbors
of her great cities are filled with silt and not one stone
of ancient Tyre or Sidon remains upon another.

But the Phoenicians had their day, brief though it was.
After they had freed themselves from Egypt they became
the leading merchants of the Mediterranean. Their vessels,
some seventy feet long, plied the trade routes which linked
Egypt, Babylonia and the Near East with Italy, Greece,
and Spain. The great ships built for the run to Tarshish in
southwest Spain were the East Indiamen of the day. Even

the Greeks envied them their naval discipline and skill. But the Phoenicians, ever mindful of their monopoly, guarded well their knowledge of winds and currents and kept their trade routes secret. Sometimes other traders would try to follow them, but seldom with success. Usually other sailors did not even dare venture as far as they did. In fact it is said that one of their fleets sailed completely around Africa two thousand years before Vasco da Gama. Their wealth increased and they founded colonies and trading posts in what are now Malta, Marseilles and Cadiz. Carthage (Tunisia now), which later gave Rome serious rivalry, was a Phoenician settlement.

From Africa the Phoenicians brought ivory; from Spain, tin and silver. The spices, perfumes and incense of the Arabian caravans passed through their hands on the way to the West. They bought from everybody and sold to everybody. They trafficked in everything, even in people, for one of their greatest businesses was the slave trade. In addition to distributing the wares of others, they were great manufacturers themselves. They made weapons of Cyprian iron and copper; they fabricated jewelry and ornaments;

having learned glassmaking in Egypt they made vases and crystal ware. But there was one product they originated themselves, and in this they had a monopoly. It was crimson dye. Somehow they had discovered that a certain shell fish contained a tiny particle of bright red coloring matter. This was enough to start the Phoenicians on a new line of business. The fish were gathered by the millions; they were crushed; and textiles were dyed in the crimson fluid. This was the origin of royal purple, which was not the purple we know, but a kind of red. Tyrian purple, it was frequently called, and the city of Tyre profited by the name.

From the standpoint of the Phoenicians the making of
this dye was their most important work, but from our standpoint there was something of much greater importance. It
so happened that the Phoenicians did a very large papyrus
business, mostly from Byblos, Phoenicia's religious capital.
So renowned was Byblos for its papyrus trade that later
on the Greeks used its name as their word for book—*biblos*
—and from that comes our word Bible. The merchants
of Byblos went to Egypt for their papyrus. They bought it
to sell, but in so doing they learned to use it themselves,
and also to use the Egyptian characters for their writing.

Hieratic	PHŒNICIAN		*Hieratic*	PHŒNICIAN	

The step between Egyptian and Phoenician writing is one which, even after the many years of study it has received, is not entirely clear. One man has proved to his own satisfaction that every Phoenician character came from a corresponding hieratic sign. We saw some of the resemblances in the preceding chart. Another scholar has maintained that the Phoenician and Egyptian writing systems are separate offshoots from a more ancient system used by all the Mediterranean countries. Still others have pointed to the fascinating scripts of Crete, which lies like a stepping-stone at the doorsill of Greece.

About two thousand years before Christ, long before the Phoenicians, the people of Crete began building great palaces, factories, and pottery works. Their culture is called Minoan, after King Minos, whose wife bore the Minotaur, the half-bull, half-man monster slain by Theseus. Minoan artists produced some of the finest paintings and sculpture of antiquity. Then, starting in the fifteenth century B.C., came a series of catastrophes. Tremendous earthquakes tumbled down the palaces and Crete was invaded, first by the Mycenaeans from the mainland of Greece and then by the Dorians, a northern people who overran Greece and the nearby Mediterranean islands. Though the flame of Minoan civilization flared up between calamities, it could not withstand them forever. By 1150 B.C., perhaps earlier, the candle had sputtered out.

The Minoans used two scripts, known today as Linear A and Linear B. Linear A dates from before 1700 B.C. and is primarily ideographic; while Linear B, which developed out of Linear A during the fourteenth and thirteenth centuries B.C., is primarily phonetic.

Minoan writing defeated all attempts at translation until 1952 when Michael Ventris, a young English architect, deciphered Linear B. With no bilingual Rosetta Stone to help him, Ventris made brilliant use of code-

breaking techniques to prove that the eighty-odd signs in
the script stand for different syllables in a primitive form
of Greek. He had discovered the language of the Mycenaeans—of Agamemnon, Achilles, and Odysseus, the
conquerors of Troy!

The idea of using signs to stand for sounds may well
have come to Crete from Egypt or the Near East. Indeed,
some scholars feel that the older Linear A is a Semitic language. Important as the two Minoan scripts are in the his-

tory of writing, however, neither stands in the direct line
of development of our own alphabet. Linear B does not
appear to have been used after 1200 B.C. When the
Greeks learned to write again, it was with Phoenician
characters.

By the time the Phoenicians were forming their alphabet, many of the inland peoples of the Near East, such as
the Assyrians, the Babylonians, and the Hittites, were using a writing system of wedge-shaped characters that were
modifications of earlier pictures or hieroglyphics. While
the *cuneiform* characters in the systems just mentioned
stood for ideas rather than sounds, at least one cuneiform
alphabet existed. It was developed some two centuries
prior to the Phoenician alphabet at Ugarit, the capital of
a small kingdom on the Mediterranean coast, north of
Phoenicia. It seems likely that the Phoenicians borrowed
from the Ugaritic alphabet and perhaps from some early
noncuneiform alphabets as well.

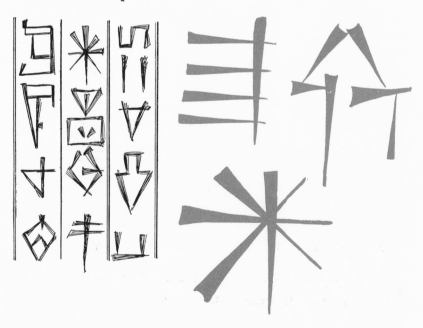

We do know that the Phoenicians had some letters which resembled those of other eastern peoples. It may be that the form of their letter *aleph*, which became the Greek *alpha* and later our *A*, came from a Babylonian character representing the face and horns of an ox, for the Phoenician word *aleph* meant "ox" and the letter was made to look like an ox's head. But it is also possible that *aleph* came from the Egyptian character for *apis*, the sacred bull. As a sound, of course, we know from our study of Egyptian writing that *A* is related to the picture-word *eagle*.

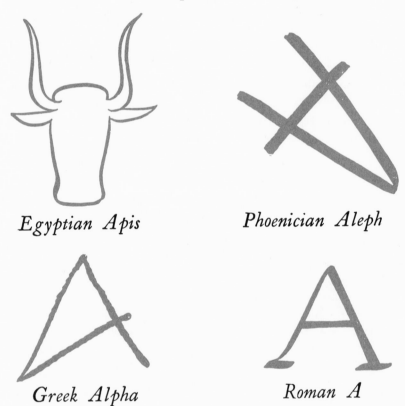

Egyptian Apis   *Phoenician Aleph*

Greek Alpha   *Roman A*

And that is about all we know of the true source, or sources, of the Phoenician letter forms.

In comparison with the Egyptians, the Phoenicians were mere upstarts. History plays odd jokes sometimes, and it seems a prank that the first to use our alphabet should be a people with no literature at all.

The Phoenicians continued to simplify and to carry writing wherever they went. They didn't improve the letters much, and in fact they were often careless in their writing for they cared nothing for the beauty or precise forms of the characters.

What is really important is that they dropped the picture-signs of the hieroglyphics altogether and retained only the sound-symbols, the part which was true alphabet. The Phoenician letters were for the most part simple in form, easy to write, and clear and easy to read.

The two great Phoenician cities of Tyre and Sidon on the eastern shore of the Mediterranean, despite their having been only twenty miles apart, each developed a separate style of writing, a separate alphabet, though both were from the same original and each had many characters similar to those of the other. The alphabet of Tyre was the one that was used chiefly by the inland tribes of Moab and Syria; and, more important for us, it was the one that the Greeks borrowed and made their own shortly after the time of the Trojan war.

This alphabet probably developed about the twelfth century B.C. when Tyre was at the height of its influence in the Mediterranean world. At that time the skill and cleverness of the men of Tyre had spread their fame through many lands. In the Old Testament we read that Solomon contracted with Hiram, king of Tyre, to assist him in the building of the Temple, as there were none more skilled at hewing timbers than these Phoenicians. And in II Chronicles 2:14 it says: ". . . his father was a man of Tyre, skillful to work in gold, and in silver, in brass, in iron, in stone, and in timber, in purple, in blue, and in fine linen, and in crimson."

The writing of the men of Tyre was borrowed by the Israelites, and the modern Hebrew letters as well as our own are descended from the practical alphabet which these Phoenician people perfected a thousand years before the birth of Christ. Some of the many alphabets which were derived from it are indicated in the chart.

One of the finest specimens of Phoenician writing, and

Phoenician
- Aramean
  - Hebrew
  - Syriac
  - Mongolian
  - Arabic
  - Pehlevi
  - Armenian
  - Georgian
- Sabœan
  - Ethiopic
    - Amharic
  - Indian
    - Pali
      - Corean
      - Burmese
      - Siamese
      - Javanese
      - Singalese
    - Nagari
      - Tibetan
      - Kashmir
      - Gujarati
      - Marathi
      - Bengali
      - Malayan
    - Dravidian
      - Tamel
      - Canarese
- Hellenic
  - Greek
  - Latin
  - Russian
  - Coptic

also the oldest known one that can be dated, is an inscription
in the alphabet of Tyre written in the reign of Mesha, king
of Moab, early in the ninth century B.C. This inscription
on a stone tablet with a rounded top known as the Moabite
stone, was discovered in 1868 in the vicinity of the Dead
Sea and is now in the museum of the Louvre in Paris. It is
quite as famous in its way as the Rosetta stone found in
Egypt, though it was easier to read because the letters so
nearly resemble the Greek.

One interesting thing in its history is that it was almost lost after it was found. As soon as the neighboring Arabs learned that the stone was valued by the Christians, they began to fight over it; and the monument that had withstood the weather and the accidents of 2700 years was broken by them into forty pieces by being heated and having water poured over it. Fortunately some copies had been made before it was broken, and the stone was partially restored and patched together.

Although it is possible that the origin of the Phoenician alphabet may never be completely determined, we already know enough of it to know that it is an important step in the road from picture writing to our twenty-six letters. When the ancient traders from Tyre carried their writing to the peninsula of Greece, about nine hundred years before Christ, they probably did not realize they were making the most important contribution of their people to the progress of civilization.

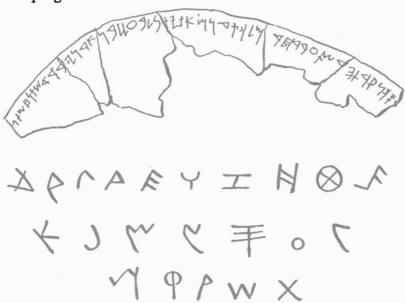

Chapter 4

THE GREEKS

Three peninsulas jut down into the Mediterranean. Upon each one in turn grew up a people which became the greatest of its day. The peninsula of Greece was the home of Athens, Sparta and Corinth. The Italian peninsula was the backbone of the Roman Empire. From the Spanish peninsula an empire spread into the Americas.

Of these Greece had the smallest empire but the greatest glory and influence.

A map of this tiny country, hardly the size of Alabama, shows the general outline, but it cannot show the hundreds of islands and islets that dot the sea. Nor can it show how there were at least three Greeces. There was a Greece of before history. There was the Greece of the days of Pericles. And there is the Greece of today.

While Crete was rich and prosperous, rival cities sprang up on the mainland of Greece itself, Mycene and Tiryns. They flourished from fifteen hundred to eleven hundred years before Christ. This was the age which Homer described in the *Iliad*. It was in Mycenae, "a well-built city and abounding in gold," that Agamemnon lived. Its art, architecture, and civilization were very much like that of Crete and its writing was Linear B. This system was used

GREECE

almost exclusively for record-keeping. As noted before, Linear B doesn't seem to have been used after 1200 B.C.—about the time the Dorians invaded Greece.

The ancient Greece we all know best is the later Greece of Pericles, when the Parthenon stood in all its perfection, and Phidias was at work with the sculpture and bas-reliefs which were to become the "classics."

Pericles

This Greece was in no sense a nation united like our own. It was merely a collection of some hundred and fifty communities. Most of these were very small, and Athens itself had only as many inhabitants as the present Albany, New York. They were constantly fighting and bickering amongst themselves, but they were united in at least one respect: their language was national except for local accents. Their alphabets, too, were pretty much the same.

It must be remembered that the truly great time for Greece, as a nation, was not this period when the sculpture and architecture that is in so many of our museums today was being produced. This was actually the beginning of

Greek decline. The earlier times, when there was more honesty and less "finish," were the really important years.

It was four centuries before Pericles, nine hundred or more years before Christ, that the alphabet took root in Greece. Of course, what the Greeks used of the Phoenician letters was hardly a finished alphabet.

The Phoenicians, we believe, supplied the Greeks with sixteen characters—all consonants, no vowels. They wrote entirely with consonants, and it was up to the reader to decide where a vowel sound was intended and which one was needed. It was a sort of "abbreviation" writing. We sometimes do almost the same thing as, for instance, yr for "your" and bldg for "building."

Later Greek

Minoan Sculpture

It so happens that Phoenician, or more properly Semitic tongues, can be written this way without confusion. Old Hebrew was written much in that fashion. However, since English is basically a vowel-sound language, it cannot be recorded with consonants alone. If we wrote English that way we should have to do too much guessing. This is how that last sentence would read: "F w wrt nglsh tht wy w shld hv t d t mch gssng." Also, while the system was satisfactory for Phoenician business records, it was not adequate for the more literate Greeks.

The Greeks developed their alphabet by changing various unused Phoenician consonant characters into the vowel letters which they needed. By adding some of their own, they eventually made a standard alphabet of twenty-four characters, not including several that were used for a while and then dropped.

Some of our letters were not present, *C* and *V* for example, because the Greek tongue did not require them. Some were used with different sound values, such as their *H* (*eta*) which stood for our long *E* and their *P* (*rho*) which had the sound of our *R*.

Many irregularities were followed by the Greeks in developing their letters. The forms were not exactly fixed and even the direction of writing could be reversed.

The Greek scribes straightened out the latter problem. Right-handed people can write much easier with a pen from left to right; but among the earliest Greek inscriptions (and a few of the early Latin ones) some of the writing goes from right to left, some from left to right, in some cases both ways alternately, and in still others, up and down. Apparently the way the writing best fit into the space determined the direction.

Writing which went in both directions was called "boustrophedon" which means "ox-turning." As an ox plows

RIGHT TO LEFT

ΠΡΩΤΟΥ

ΓΑΡ ΜΕΥ

BOUSTRO-PHEDON

ΠΡΩΤΟΥ

ΜΕΥ ΓΑΡ

LEFT TO RIGHT

ΠΡΩΤΟΥ

ΜΕΥ ΓΑΡ

a furrow it turns and then goes in the other direction. This meant that all but the symmetrical letters, such as Π and H and M, had to be reversed in alternate lines of writing. For the sake of simplicity and uniformity, the practice of going from left to right was agreed upon by the sixth century B.C., about a hundrd years before the time of Pericles.

If you were to place the Moabite stone, with its ninth-century B.C. Phoenician or Semitic characters, next to the oldest Greek inscriptions that we know (also from the

eighth or ninth century B.C.), and then if you could place
next to those the oldest writing of the Romans (from before the fifth century B.C.), you would be surprised that
they are so much alike. The letters which have become our
A, our *D*, our *E*, our *H*, *K*, *M*, *N*, *O*, and *Q*, would all
look very similar in these alphabets from the Middle East,
from Greece and from Italy, widely separated in space and
many years apart in time.

One important thing they have in common: they are, in
each case, the crude, *beginning* alphabet. The Greeks
set the shapes of the letters, so that they were no longer
variable marks but well-formed characters. Their alphabet was fully developed by the fifth century before Christ.
The Romans made them beautiful and suitable for writing.

Here it might be a good idea to take time out to see just
how some of the letters have developed from the time that
they were actual pictures.

The Phoenicians picked up an assortment of picture
characters from which they fashioned their letters. In
some cases they disregarded the original meaning and sound
of the character—simply took the picture, gave it a name
in their own language, then made a letter of it. The names
of most of the characters were common objects, such as ox,
house, camel, door, and so on. With a little imagination,
one can see the original object in a good many of the letters.

One thing which is sometimes not very clear is that a
letter may have had several roots. The sound perhaps may
be from one picture-word while the shape may be from
another. Two different picture-words may be simplified to
look pretty much alike and thus cause some question as to
which is actually the original of the letter. Even the experts
on these things do not agree exactly at all times. Here is
the generally accepted way in which some of the Greek
letters evolved.

We saw in the last chapter the steps by which the Greek *alpha* (the ancestor of our modern *A*) evolved in turn from the Phoenician *aleph*, and the Babylonian sign for *ox* or the Egyption hieroglyph for *bull*.

The Phoenicians possibly got their *daleth* from the Egyptian hieroglyph that originally meant "door" and looked like a door with panels:

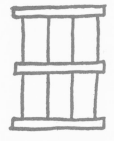

The simpler Egyptian symbol:

became in the hieratic script:

The Phoenicians wrote it:

and the Greeks:

The letter which is now our *H* had the name *cheth*, meaning "fence." The character on the Moabite stone does in fact look like a fence section:

In early Greek it was written thus:

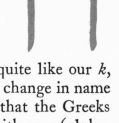

and finally by the Greeks and by ourselves like this:

The Greek *kappa*, in form and sound quite like our *k*, was taken from the Phoenician *kaph*. The change in name may be accounted for simply by the fact that the Greeks ended the names of many of their letters with an *a* (alph*a*, bet*a*, gamm*a*, and so on).

Kaph meant "palm of the hand" and was at first a realistic picture word:

The Phoenicians wrote it:

and the Greeks modified that sign
only slightly:

but when they began to write
from left to right, they flipped
it over to make:

The Hebrews interpreted the meaning as "fist" and so
wrote it with a symbol which looked more like a partly
closed hand:

Lambda, the Greek forerunner of our letter *L*, came
from *lamed*, the Phoenician word-sign for "whip," which

in some way developed from a hieroglyph. The Phoenicians wrote the sign:

and the Greeks made it:

It had to be turned on its side to become the Roman *L*.

The Egyptian hieroglyph for water,

and the hieroglyph for owl,

became the Phoenician *mem:*

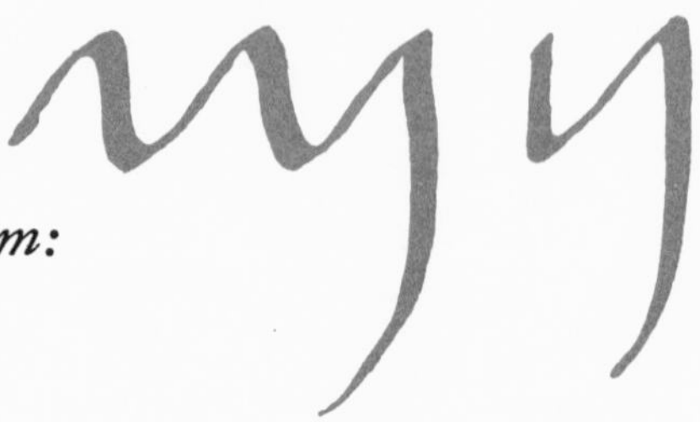

Mem became Greek *mu* (*M*):

We have here a chart showing the nineteen characters that the Greeks took from the Phoenician traders. The second column shows the early Greek alphabet developed from them, plus the original characters which were added.

PHŒNICIAN		GREEK	
aleph		alpha	
beth		beta	
gimel		gamma	
daleth		delta	
he		epsilon	
zayin		zeta	
cheth		eta	
teth		theta	
yod		iota	
kaph		kappa	
lamed		lambda	
mem		mu	
nun		nu	
sameth		xá	
ayin		omicron	
pe		pí	
resh		rho	
shin		sigma	
tau		tau	
		upsilon	
		phí	
		chí	
		psí	
		omega	

This Greek alphabet was officially adopted by Athens in 403 B.C. Little by little it spread over all of Greece. It is used almost intact in Greece today, and you would find the headlines of any Greek newspaper written in the same letters that were used by Pericles himself. Compare this modern Greek alphabet set in printer's type with the Athenian alphabet in the chart on page 95.

ΑΒΓΔΕΖΗΘΙΚΛΜΝΞΟΠΡΣΤΥΦΧΨΩ

Thirteen of these letters (the basic alphabet) were later taken over in the same form by the Romans and are still used in our alphabet today. These letters are shown here as they appeared in the stylus-drawn alphabet, which was the characteristic method of Greek writing. Compare these thirteen with their modern counterparts used today.

In spite of the great beauty of Greek writing, two things make it appear strange to us. Like all ancient writing it is all in capitals; small letters were not introduced until the Middle Ages. In the second place there is no space between words. Printed this way this paragraph would read:

INSPITEOFTHEGREATBEAUTYOFGREEK
WRITINGTWOTHINGSMAKEITAPPEAR
STRANGETOUSLIKEALLANCIENTWRITING
ITISALLINCAPITALSSMALLLETTERSWERE
NOTINTRODUCEDUNTILTHEMIDDLEAGES

Punctuation came later (very slowly, it is true) as literature advanced, and the writing masters became more than
simple clerks or recorders. All these elements of our
present-day forms, such as capitals and paragraphs and
variations in size and handling, are refinements of which
the early Greeks were not aware.

One of the earliest bits of Greek papyrus writing still
preserved is from the fourth century B.C. Notice how even
the lettering is, how controlled and handsome the characters are.

ΓᶜΝΤΡΕΤΗΜΑΦΑΤ
ΙᴖΚΑΤΑ ͼΚΑᛞΑΙΔ
ΤΑΜΕΝΗΛΙΚΑᴖᴧ
ᵒᵞΚᴊᵒΓᴉͼͼᵒΓᵒΡΕͳΤᵒ

The Greeks also used a tablet and stylus. The tablet was
simply a section of wood with a raised rim, like a shallow
pan, containing a coating of wax. The stylus was a pointed
instrument of metal or ivory. The writer scratched his letters into the wax with the point of his stylus. To erase

what had been written, he scraped the wax away or melted it slightly until the surface was again smooth. Such a tablet was handy and cheap. It was used in school rooms and for letters, notices, and memoranda.

The character of the tools, as in all other cases that we have seen, gave a particular character to the letters. The lines were mostly straight and all the strokes of about the same weight. We shall see later how the Romans put curves into the letters and developed the handsome "thick and thin" character of the alphabet, but the tools of the Greeks did not permit this. As the stylus was pushed through the soft surface of the tablet, it tended to collect the wax on its point. The lines therefore were irregular and necessarily short, since the stylus had to be lifted often to remove the waste wax from the point.

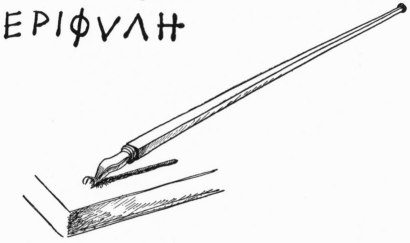

Papyrus writing, while regular and "pen-like," had, in the beginning, many of these stylus characteristics.

Although the Greeks never developed a real written script, they did, as they wrote faster and with more freedom, outgrow square letters of straight lines and introduce some curves. This is shown in these letters, freely rewritten from a bit of papyrus of about the third century B.C.

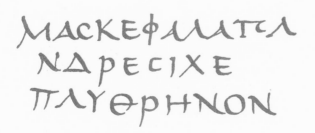

Besides papyrus, the Greeks had another material, parchment, which was used for permanent documents and books.

The development of parchment had a great effect on the alphabet right down to the Middle Ages. It was first used as early as 500 B.C., but only one side could be written on. About 200 B.C., the story goes, Ptolemy V, king of Egypt, forbade the shipping of papyrus out of the country because the reed from which it was made was in danger of becoming extinct. Faced with this shortage, a young student scribe in Pergamus, an ancient city in Asia Minor, tried to find a substitute for papyrus.

He discovered that by splitting the skin of a kid, goat, or sheep, bleaching it, and pounding and finishing it by rubbing, he had a wonderful surface to write on. It was smooth; it took and held the ink without blurring; and it could be rolled up and would keep, it seemed, almost forever. We call the improved skin *parchment* from the city of Pergamus where it was first used.

The beautifully smooth surface allowed still other refinements to come into the Greek alphabet. The Greek scribes became artists. However, we cannot tell so much as we should like to about the effect of this new parchment on earliest writing, for the oldest example of parchment

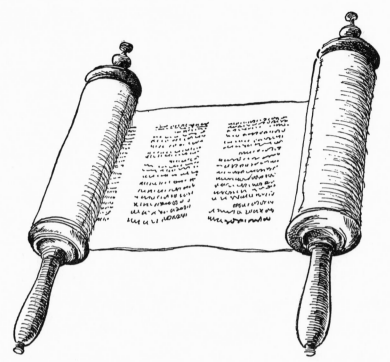

used in a Greek book is a copy of Homer from the third or fourth century after Christ.

Eventually, by the fourth century of the Christian era, the sheets of parchment were bound together in the form of a book as we know it, but to the Greeks and Romans until a very late period a "book" meant a "roll."

In addition to all the other things the early Greeks contributed to our alphabet, they gave us the word itself. It is, of course, composed of the names of the first two letters: *alpha* and *beta*—alphabet!

The ancient Greeks were an imaginative and artistic people. They developed a culture superior even to that of the Egyptians in many ways. In their hands the borrowed alphabet was improved and developed and passed on to the Romans from whom we have taken our letters directly.

Chapter 5

THE ROMANS

Rome grew from a little inland "cross roads" town on the Tiber River to a great empire extending her conquests to all the known world and drawing tribute from colonies as far away as England and Egypt. As a country she had no special natural advantages, but her people were great organizers and great warriors, and from them sprang great leaders. Like the Phoenicians, the Romans knew how to borrow and adapt to their own uses the best that had been developed by others. The more they conquered the more they brought back.

One of the things Rome borrowed first was the alphabet, and she borrowed that long before she did any conquering to speak of. When Romulus and Remus, fabled founders of the city, were still running wild with their foster-mother wolf, fine up-to-date cities of the Greeks were thriving upon the lower portion of the Italian peninsula, as far north as Naples. It would be natural to suppose that the rugged Romans merely took over the Greek alphabet in south Italy, as they took over the Greek cities and territories there. Scholars used to believe that the Romans got their letters from their neighbors to the south. Now, however, we know that this is only partly true. There was a little country up north of Rome that had a hand in the matter.

That was Etruria, the country of the Etruscans. We know very little about them. They left behind pottery, jewels, and arches of what must have been magnificent buildings. Their language, however, is still one of mystery, for only a couple of hundred words have been deciphered. It is thought that Etruria began to rise about a thousand years before Christ. For several centuries she was the great-

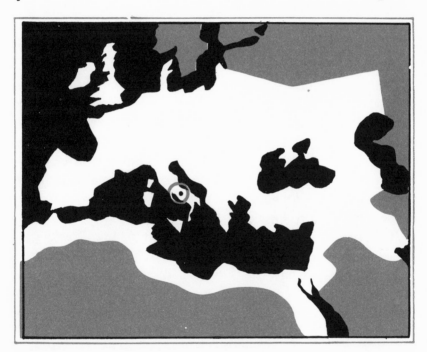

ROME
HER EMPIRE IN A.D. 100

est military power in Italy, sometimes fighting against the Greeks and sometimes with them. At last, soon after the time of Pericles in Greece, she was beaten by the Romans and, like most Roman victims, disappeared completly.

The Etruscans got their alphabet from the Greeks— from the Greeks in Asia Minor, it is thought. Thus the primitive Romans were practically surrounded by the Greek alphabet. It was used by the Greeks to the south of them, by the Etruscans to the north. More exactly, the Etruscans were not only north of them but *upon* them, for in the early days Etruria ruled Rome, and the first kings of Rome were Etruscans.

Although Rome's golden age came hundreds of years after the age of Pericles in Greece, Rome began using the Greek alphabet long before the decline of Greece. It was about 700 B.C., when Etruria was powerful in Italy, that the letters were taken by the Romans. That was three hundred years *before* the Greek alphabet was officially adopted at Athens, and only about a hundred years after the alphabet was brought to Greece.

This means of course that to some extent the Greeks and the Romans were working out their alphabets *at the same time*. It means that the Romans did not take over the alphabet at the point where the Greeks had finished—as described in the last chapter; it was still crude when they began to use it. This chart shows the Roman letters that were taken directly from Greek letters, either letters that were then in use or letters that the Greeks had dropped.

Even the very ancient custom of boustrophedon writing still persisted when the Romans began to write. In several early Latin inscriptions there are examples of this system.

Besides changing the characters themselves, the Romans varied the alphabet of Greece by adding some letters and discarding others. The standard Greek alphabet had

Greek		Latin	
A	A	A	A
B	B	B	C G
Γ	Γ	C	D
Δ	D	D	E
E F	E F	E	F
Ι	Z	F	
Θ	H	H	H
K	I K	I	I K
Λ M	Λ M	K	L
N	N	L	M
O Γ	O Π	M	N
Φ R	Φ P	N	O
E T	S	O	P
Y Ξ	T Y X	Q R	Q
		S T	R S T
		V X	V Y
			X Z

twenty-four letters; the standard late Roman alphabet had twenty-three; ours has twenty-six.

From the standard Greek alphabet the Romans took A, B, E, Z, H, I, K, M, N, O, T, X and Y with hardly any change at all. The letter B, for instance was merely a rounded form of the Greek character. Remodeling and finishing other Greek letters, the Romans produced C (and G), L, S, P, R, D and V. F and Q were taken from two old characters abandoned by the Greeks themselves. And that makes twenty-three.

Meanwhile you may have been wondering why Z comes at the end of the alphabet, for with the Greeks it had been number six. At first the Romans dropped Z entirely, then found they could not get along without it. When they allowed Z to return to the alphabet, it had lost its place in the regular order and had to get to the end of the line. We have kept Z there ever since.

The three missing letters, J, U and W, were not used by the Romans at all. U and W developed from V about a thousand years ago, and J developed from the letter I about five hundred years ago.

Besides finally establishing the order and content of the alphabet, the Romans greatly increased the beauty of the letter forms themselves.

The square corners and sharp angles of the Greek letters gave way, in many cases, to gradual curves and graceful shapes in Latin usage.

The Greek letters, of course, were shaped as they were because they developed during the time of wax-tablet writing. The Roman letters, likewise, became more flowing and graceful because, as we shall see, they were developed by another kind of writing tool.

For the first time, perhaps, we shall notice in Roman letters that all the strokes are not of the same weight; some are thick, some are thin, and the curves show a gradual change from thick to thin. This characteristic was not necessarily designed; it, like the more flowing shape of the letters, came about because the tools which were used in developing the letters gave them that character *naturally*.

The Roman alphabet was developed through *writing* as compared to DRAWING.

As the Roman legions conquered more and more of the world, it became the custom for generals and Caesars and emperors to erect triumphal arches and memorial columns to make certain that their names and brave deeds would live in the memories of men. These monuments were covered with sculptures and relief carvings. Along with carved illustrations went inscriptions, and the cutting of the letters came to be a fine art. In fact, the vain conquerors would accept nothing less than the very best work.

ABCDE
FHILM
NOPQR
STVXR

Stone doesn't seem, at first thought, to be a surface that would encourage flowing lines and graceful curves or the development of writing characteristics. Others before the Romans had carved letters on stone and they had been usually stiff and harsh. How then did the Romans succeed in giving this written quality to their letters? The only possible answer is that they *were* written before they were carved. The carving was done merely to make the huge letters permanent. After the outlines made by the original artist-writer, or letterer, had been carved out carefully with the chisel, they were gone over and filled in with paint to

make them look like the original writing. Now the paint has been worn away by hundreds of years of wind and rain, of heat and cold, but the beautiful forms remain.

There really is no other way to explain the shapes of the Roman capitals. If they had been designed with rulers and compasses, instead of written with a free hand, the swells of the curves, the different "weights" or thicknesses of

horizontal and vertical and oblique strokes, the whole *char-acter* of the letters would have been different. They would have had a geometric sameness. Only free-hand strokes could have given them the proportions and shapes and variations which they possess.

Let us look at the letter *A* as it appears on one of these Roman inscriptions. The principles governing its design will be the same for all the other letters. First we notice that none of the three lines which make it are of the same thickness—there is one thick, one thin, and one medium weight stroke. This is no accident. The handling of the tool with which it was made caused the difference.

The forms of letters throughout all the ages have been determined very largely, as we have seen already, by the tools with which they were made. The Babylonian and Assyrian cuneiform picture symbols have their peculiar character because they were made by pressing little wedges into wet clay. The Egyptian hieroglyphics were as they were because they were chiseled in relief on stone. The hieratic script looked as it did because it was written with a wide, flat reed pen. The Greek letters were square and even because they were scratched on wax with a stylus.

What instrument was used to write the huge inscriptions with such varied width of line and such controlled harmony and proportion? The answer is simple. Imagine a double-pointed drawing tool such as two sharpened pencils joined together with a rubber band and held firmly parallel to each other. When held at a set angle, they will make strokes of different widths depending upon the direction in which the stroke is made.

Here we see how the letterer can make a very thin line by holding the pencils so that one follows immediately behind the other.

He can make the width of his line vary from this to the whole distance separating the points simply by varying the direction of the stroke.

Let us look at the letter *B*. Here are both straight lines

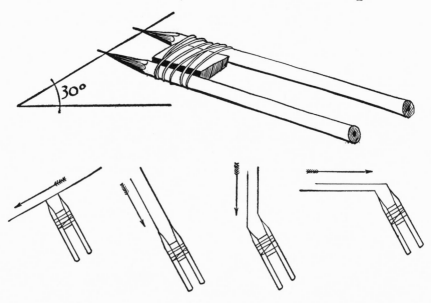

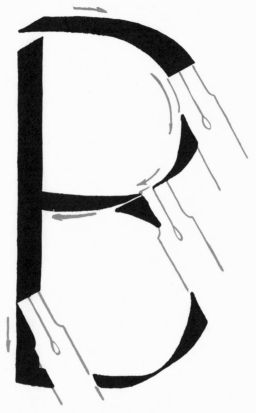

and curves. The short horizontal sections which join the curves to the stem are thinner than the vertical line because the tool is so held that the points making the outline of the letter move more nearly one behind the other for the horizontal than for the vertical strokes. The widest possible lines will be those made when the pencils are moving at right angles to the thinnest lines. These wide lines come in the *B* in the *outward* down strokes of the curves of the bowls. At the vertical the line is thinner again (medium, as it is in the vertical stem). So the lines are slightly thicker just above the center of the bowls, tapering gracefully down to their thinnest where they near the horizontal.

What kind of tool the Roman letterers used we do not know exactly, but it must have been something like these double pencils we have described. Of course, a wide, flat pen-like tool could achieve the same results. It seems likely that this method of writing or drawing a letter for an inscription was used at first to estimate the proper width of line for a certain height of letter. The artists were so pleased with this "pen-character" in the letters that they kept on until in time, this difference in weight of strokes or thickness of lines became as much a part of the alphabet as the forms of the letters themselves.

Another important contribution to the form of letters, as we now know them, especially on the printed page, was made by the Romans as a result of the way they carved their inscriptions on monuments. One sees on most letters that are drawn or printed, including the type in which this book is set, thin lines at right angles to the end of each stroke. These little lines are called *serifs*. They are finishing strokes. Their first appearance on the stone-cut capital letters of the Romans was no more accidental than the thick and thin strokes. The manuscript quill and reed gave to letters their thick-thin character. Serifs, too, had a *functional* beginning. They were the necessary finishing touches in cutting letters in stone. Even when the letters were written on parchment or paper, serifs were retained as an essential part, for they were found to give a logical finish that satisfied the eye better than square or abrupt endings of the separate strokes.

Here is how serifs probably came about. When the artist had finished writing the letters in his inscription, they looked rather like this:

Then he went over them and trimmed them up a bit so that when he turned them over to the stone carver, they looked like this:

The carver was confronted with certain problems. After the letter *I*, for instance, was cut in the stone, if it was at all large, there was an optical illusion which tended to make it look narrower at the ends than it did in the middle.

To avoid this the stone carver made it just a little wider at the ends—spread the stroke just a bit.

Now when he had finished his cutting from top to bottom, he found he had to clean up any rough stone left at the ends. The best way to do this was to come into the main stroke from the side.

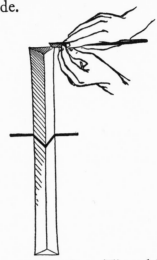

It was a delicate operation. The chisel could so easily slip and ruin the whole inscription. To avoid this the carver started the finishing out a little to the right of the main cut and let it extend a little to the left. After the straight end was cut, he rounded it off into the stem, and a very beautiful and logical finish for the letter came into being.

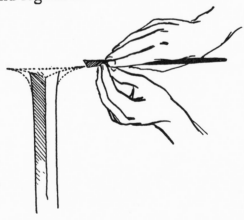

This serif was so valuable mechanically, and so handsome artistically, that it became a real part of the letter form. The manuscript writer found, just as the carver had, that a stroke without a serif looked unfinished. So the serif has continued to be a part of the letter ever since.

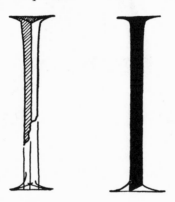

No finer Roman capital letters are to be seen anywhere than those inscribed on a stone tablet on the pedestal of the great column erected by the Emperor Trajan in Rome about the year 113 of the Christian era. The simple harmony of the lines and curves and the grace and good taste of the fine proportions have caused them to serve as models for more than eighteen hundred years. While the letters *J*, *U*, and *W* were not members of the Roman alphabet, they are drawn in the style of the Trajan alphabet and included with it here to make it complete.

It is indeed thrilling to look at these capitals, for they have the very breath of free artistry in them. Many designers have tried to determine a way to a better set of proportions. Many changes in the shape have been tried. Many mechanical methods of writing and drawing have been invented. But no one has yet succeeded in making a Roman capital alphabet which is more beautiful, more easily written, more honestly arrived at than these fine old letters.

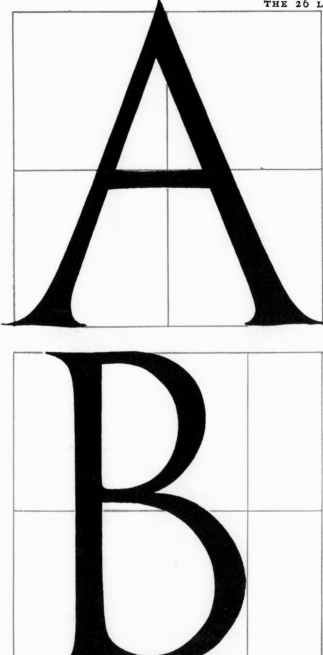

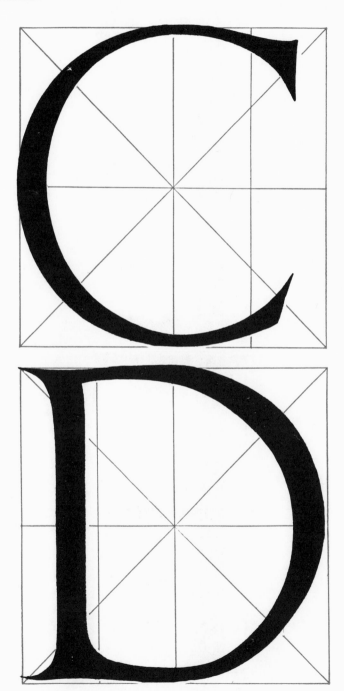

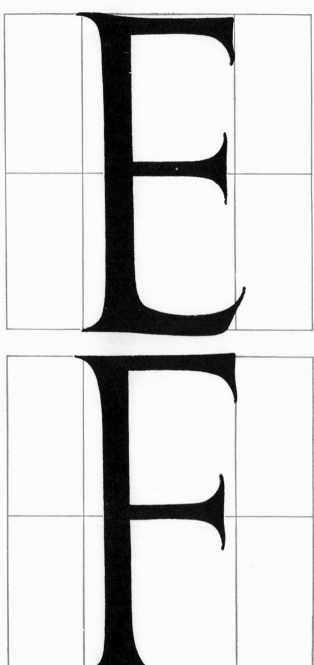

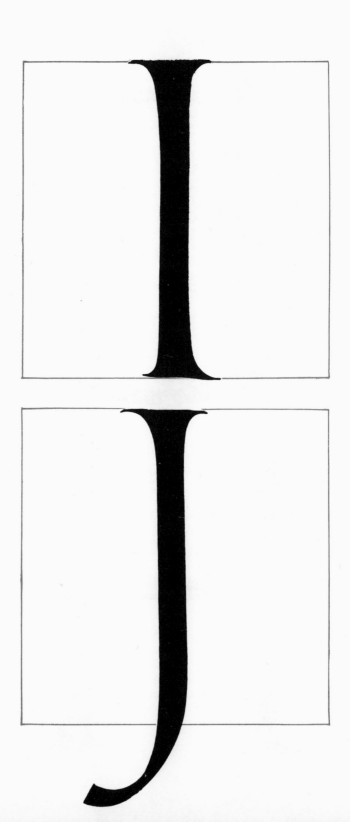

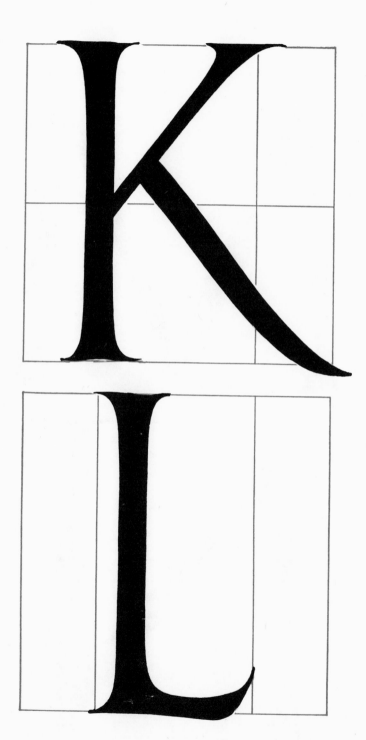

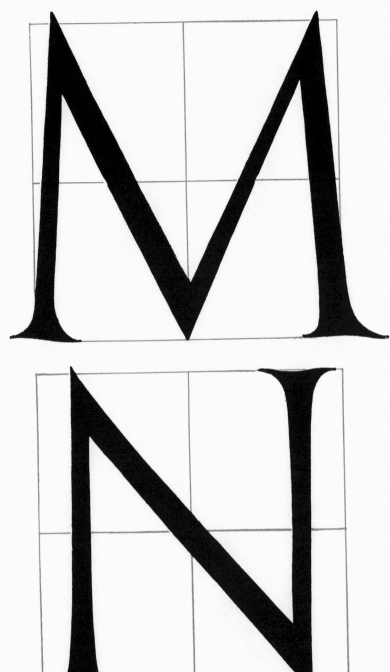

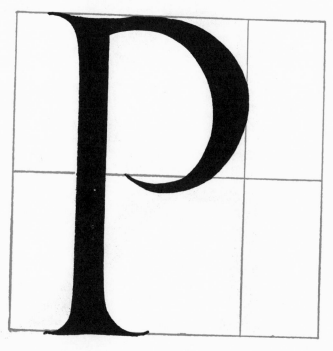

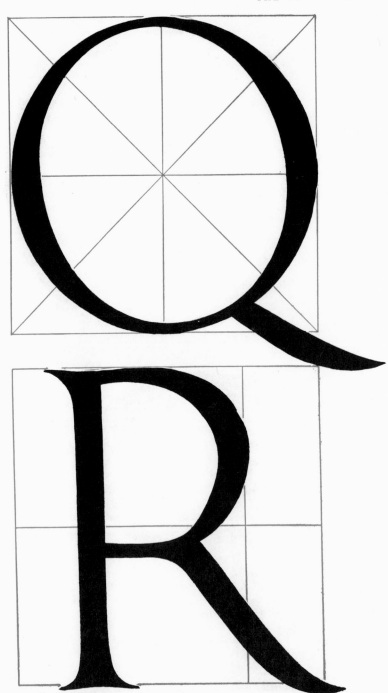

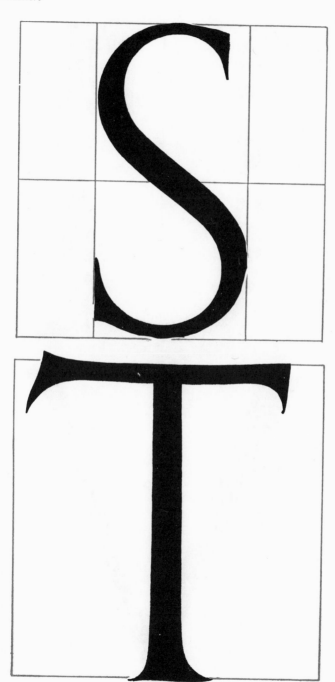

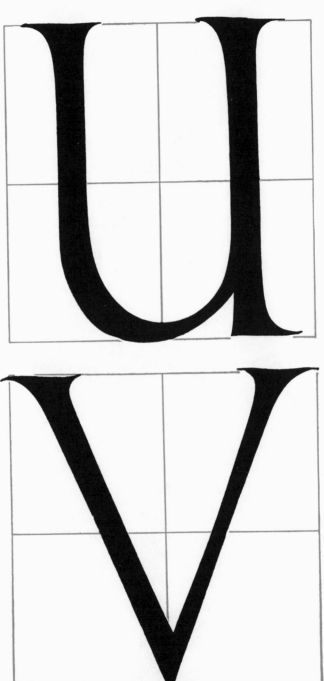

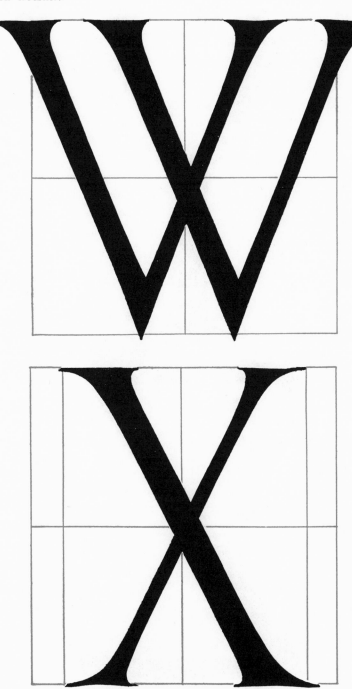

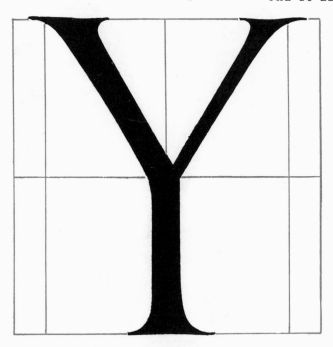

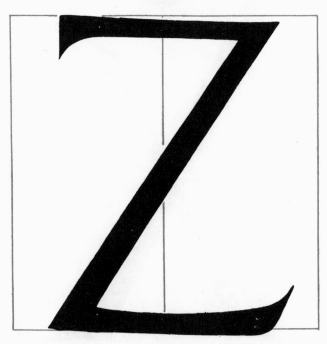

Notice that these letters, constructed with ruler and compass, while mechanically perfect,

CAES

are not nearly so beautiful as these Trajan capitals, which were *written* by the hand of an artist.

CAES

Almost anyone who admires fine letters can make acceptable capitals after a few trials if he works freely and simply as the old artists did and if he uses the right kind of tool. Perhaps that is the best way to get a real feeling for their fine proportions and their honest beauty. The amateur's letters will not be as good as the letters of the Trajan column, but that need not discourage him too much. Many professionals are unable to write them, too!

The Roman capitals, then, reached their final form through the influence of the double-edged writing tool and the carver's chisel in the hands of skilled craftsmen.

With the increased use of pen and paper for writing and the increase in the amount of writing itself, in books and documents and proclamations, professional writers made their appearance in the Roman Empire. There were, of

STATILIO
CASSIOLONGINO
COS·XI·OCTOBR

course, many people who could not write at all, and others who wrote very badly. When a person had a message to be written, he called in a scribe to do it for him, just as today one goes to a printer to have something set up in type. The professional scribes became very able; they could write with great speed and with almost perfect regularity.

NO·AVG·GERMANICO· X̄V̄

At first the scribes were careful to follow exactly the forms of the letters as they had appeared for years on monuments and buildings. As they became more familiar with their letters and their tools, however, and also more pressed for time because of increased demands for their work, they gradually drifted into a more and more *written* way of working. Their letters became real handwriting.

The Roman "Square Capitals" was the first finished style to result from this trend. The examples we have here are taken from a manuscript of the time. If you look at them carefully and compare them with the Trajan letters you will see that both alphabets are built on the same skeleton. That is, the basic forms and general proportions are the same. This can be shown most easily by laying a piece of transparent paper over an original Trajan letter and then writing that letter freely with double pencils follow-

ing the shape carefully. The result will be a "Square"
letter. In effect, this is what the Roman scribes did—they
kept the skeleton of the old letters but created a new alphabet by using a freer writing method.

The stone letters had been cleaned up with a fine chisel.
The first pen letters were finished off with a pointed pen.
In the Square alphabet everything was done with the same
flat pen. For this reason one of the most striking differences
was that the serifs now were rather wide and square instead
of little pointed wedges as they had been in the stone-cut
letters. It simply wasn't logical or natural to make a pointed
serif with a wide pen; and, since the serif was already felt
to be a necessary part of the letter, the honest thing to do
was to make a square finishing stroke with the wide pen
and let it go at that. The broad squarish serif at the end of
the left hand stroke of the *A* is a good example.

EF
GH
IJK
LM

This freely written alphabet is called a "book hand" because its chief use for many years was in manuscript books. By about the third century after Christ it was used almost everywhere for manuscript work.

But all the time that the Square letters were coming into general use, another new style was gradually being born. It grew naturally out of the Square Roman as the scribes became more skillful and speedy in their use of quill pens on parchment. The greater speed of their writing did not mean, however, that they had grown careless. They did leave off many little refining strokes. Where the serif could be made by a final turn of the pen instead of requiring a separate stroke, they did it that way. Where letters or parts of letters could be joined together or made to flow one into another without lifting the pen, they also did that. In the case of A, one entire stroke was omitted. The letters were not made less graceful or less beautiful; and, in fact, in many instances the harmony of the letters in combination with one another was increased.

The style that thus developed from the rapid writing of the scribes we now call "Rustic Capitals," perhaps because the letters have a natural simplicity. They look as if they had been casually done, although actually great skill went into their making.

The change in the general character of the letters was due partly to a new way of holding the pen. In writing the Square Roman, the scribe had held the nibs of his pen at an angle of about thirty degrees from the line of writing. That made the vertical strokes thicker than the horizontal. In making the Rustic Capitals he shifted the nibs of the pen to nearly sixty degrees so the horizontal lines became heavier than the verticals. In the illustration the diagonal line shows the position of the nibs of the pen.

The curves, naturally, became different too. The widest part of the swell changed its position. Because of this new pen position, there was a kind of pull to the right, to keep the nibs of the pen from jamming together and "sputtering." This is most obvious in such letters as *O*.

KLM
NO
PQ
RST

In addition to the kind of tools used, another important influence on the letter forms was the character of the work-man—his inherited national characteristics. The only basic changes letters underwent from the time of the Roman stone-cut inscriptions to the middle of the fifteenth century came through the influence of the quill pen working on parchment or paper, but *national* characteristics were having their effect.

Even when the same alphabet, this Trajan Roman, for instance, was written by different peoples, it showed the influence of national habits or peculiarities. In Germany there developed a characteristic style of writing which we seldom see in America. Spanish and Italian and English

German Blackletter

and Scandinavian letters all have special features that are accounted for by the nationalities of the writers.

A   N   G   L   O   S   Q   U   A   R   E

Anglo Saxon

A   F   N   U

English

A   D   E   G   O   P   Q   U

Spanish

So it was during the time that the Roman alphabet was spreading all over the world. Each nation took it from Rome and in time put into it little changes which other nations did not. You will see, if you look at manuscripts of the same period in history but written in different countries, that the letters really differ one from another.

What is more important than these individual changes, however, from the standpoint of the development of the alphabet, is that the writing was becoming much more like "handwriting" as we know it today. Although so far there was no small-letter alphabet, the Rustic Roman Capitals were pointing toward one. If we write the *E* for instance, first as it was in the Square Capitals and then keep on writing it faster and faster, we will note several strange things happening to the original letter. These things were happening all the time that the "Rustics" were developing. All the letters were becoming more and more like handwriting, more and more like small letters instead of capitals.

Just how these changes took place as the alphabet was carried to various parts of the Roman Empire and developed in different hands is in itself a fascinating story. The transformation of the letters from the sixth century down through the Middle Ages, which produced manuscript pages such as had never been seen before and have never been created since, is one of the most interesting chapters in the whole history of the alphabet.

Chapter 6

SMALL LETTERS

In the early years of the fifth century of the Christian era a boy of sixteen was captured by the Roman soldiers in Gaul and enslaved in Ireland. The boy, who had come to know the more civilized customs of the Romans, looked about him in dismay and wonder at the sad state of barbarity of the native Celts. These warlike, superstitious people were the original inhabitants of the islands before the Romans first came to their shores under the leadership of Julius Caesar in 55 B.C. Even continuous Roman rule, beginning with the invasion of southern Britain A.D. 43–47 by Claudius, did not civilize them in Britain proper. And in Ireland they were still wilder. Led by their cruel Druid priests, who held them in bondage and even demanded human sacrifices from them, they roamed the mountains of Wales and Scotland and across the sea in Ireland. There they kept their pagan ways and lived little differently than had the cave men of prehistoric times.

The boy, whose name was Saccath (or Sucat), worked for six years as a slave tending sheep in the Irish hills. He finally escaped to the coast and made his way home, but he couldn't rest for thinking of the sad state of the Irish people. He determined to dedicate his life to them and set about preparing himself for his future work by studying for the priesthood.

By that time the Romans had ceased to persecute Christians and had taken up the new religion themselves. In fact, it was they who did more than any others to spread Christianity throughout all the countries they governed and new lands they conquered.

When Saccath finished his studies and was ordained he asked to be sent to Ireland. His wish was granted, and through the good offices of St. Germanus he was made a bishop and sent on his mission. He organized the Christians who were already there and he made many new converts. The hardships and dangers he faced among these cruel and barbaric people were great, but his patience was greater and he won many over to the gentler ways of Christianity.

He established schools, and soon his pupils went out to
help others. The Pope was so pleased with his work that
he gave him the honorary name of Patricius, meaning
"noble." We know him better as Saint Patrick, the patron
saint of the country he started on its way to civilization.

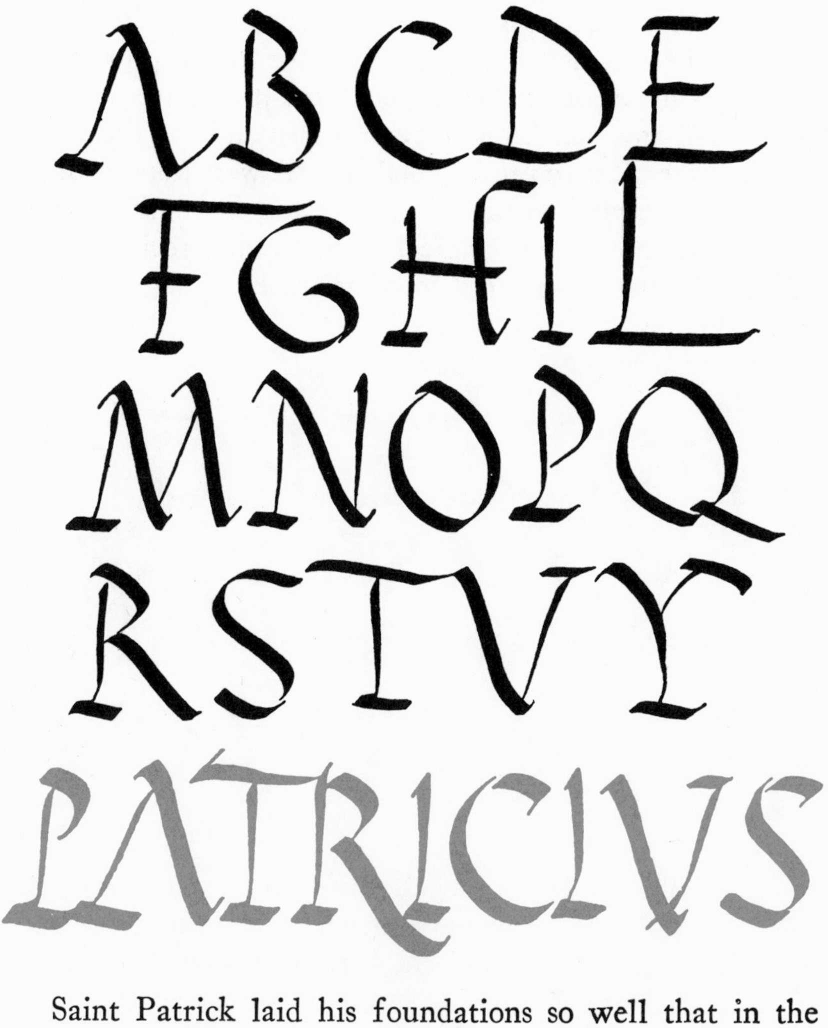

ABCDE
FGHIL
MNOPQ
RSTVY

PATRICIVS

Saint Patrick laid his foundations so well that in the following centuries his once wild and pagan country became one of the seats of learning for Europe. Perhaps the most important thing he taught the Irish was to write with Roman letters. By his time not only were Square capitals and Rustic letters well developed, but the ever-increasing amount of writing and the need for speed had started still another alphabet on its way.

The Church throughout Europe encouraged writing and was the chief employer of the scribes, for the scriptures had constantly to be copied. Then, too, more people were learning to read and there was increasing demand for the work of the scribes. These professional writers were kept at their desks from early morning until it was too dark to see. Wealthy people called for nicely written manuscript books, and scribes were also hired to write public documents and to do copying.

ABCΔEFGH
JKLMNO
PQRSTVYZ

Gradually the letters which were used for the *body* of the books and papers became somewhat more simplified and easier to write (we saw how the E changed—this happened to *all* the letters). Beginning letters of sentences and headings and very formal work, however, were still written in the old Roman Square or Rustic letters.

Adehmqt

This new writing which came into being now got the name of "uncial," perhaps because the Romans first used it for announcements or signs on which the individual letters were about an inch high (the Latin *uncialis* means "inch"). Another theory, however, is that the word came from the Latin *uncus*, which means "crooked." Compared with the letters on the Trajan Column, these uncials were indeed crooked!

Look first at the Roman uncials. These were probably very similar to the first writing which Saint Patrick's followers used in the land of the Druids. Let us observe some

400 AD · 600 AD · 1000 AD

60° · 90° · 30°

of the characteristics. The same instrument, the flat quill pen, was used as in making the Square Capitals and the Rustic letters, but the nibs were held in a more nearly horizontal position. That made all the horizontal strokes very

thin and all the vertical ones almost as wide as the pen itself. When the scribe wrote with the pen held in this way,
he pulled his letters a little out of shape in the curves.

One other main feature of this writing is that there are
no serifs. The letters were becoming more and more rapidly written, less and less formal. It was natural that serifs,
if they appeared at all, would be extremely simple. They
were nothing more than mere flicks of the quill at the ends
of strokes.

CAPITAL

small letters

We may see the dim beginnings of our small letters, or
"minuscules" as they are technically called, in the rounding of what were straight lines in the original Roman
capitals and in the tendency to extend some of the lines as
in the D and G. But the uncial was still primarily a
capital letter, or "majuscule." There were no coupling
strokes yet. In the main, there is more resemblance in their
form to capitals than to small letters. Moreover, they were
not used as small letters, for none of the Rustic or Square
letters were used with them for capitals. Sentences began

FUIT AB
INITIO ✠

Quod vidimus
oculis nostris

with uncials, not with other styles of letters, except for decorated initials, and of course there had been decorated initials before the uncials appeared.

A much more important step toward the development of small letters was the increased tendency to couple letters. This brought about a more and more written character in the letters themselves.

A further development of the uncials, the semiuncials, was coming into being. The basic type of semiuncial was a strong, beautifully designed letter, showing honestly its

dependence upon the quill. It was decorative but it was also readable. The semiuncial was, in fact, the first approach to small-letter writing and the father of all small letters which were to come.

The semiuncials, like all the other letters we have seen, were given a certain national character by every people who used them. The Irish scribes made the most of them and developed them into the most beautiful manuscript hand that has ever been seen. This Irish style of writing was so delicate and so highly finished that it became the most famous of all the semiuncials.

The Irish letters shown here are taken from the *Book of Kells*, which is called by most experts the handsomest manuscript book ever written. This book is an illuminated copy (that is, decorated with colored initial letters and designs in the margins) of the Gospels in Latin written some time in the seventh century in a monastery at Kells in County Meath, Ireland. The book also contains local records dating from the eighth century. It has been preserved through these centuries and may now be seen in the library of Trinity College, Dublin.

So beautiful is the book and so impressed were people by it that some time after it was written a legend grew up about its origin. As the story goes, more than a hundred years after Saint Patrick had brought the Roman handwriting to Ireland, two monks named Columba and Finnian (now known as Saint Columba and Saint Finnian) vied with each other in good works and in the production of beautiful manuscript books. Saint Finnian was very proud of a psalter which he treasured beyond price. Saint Columba resolved to copy that book and to make his copy even more beautiful.

For this purpose, Columba went to visit Saint Finnian. He was determined to copy the book by stealth and so

abcde
fghilm
nopqr
stux7

surprise his friend with a finer copy than the original. He found where Saint Finnian kept his masterpiece and carried it off to his cell after everyone had retired. There he labored each night, taking the precious book back to its accustomed place before morning.

At first he worked under great difficulties, for by candle light the colors of the decorations and initial letters did not look the same as they did by daylight. But a miracle

came to help him. A beam of strong white light came down
through the ceiling to light his page, while the rest of the
cell was in comparative darkness.

Everything went well and the book grew in perfection and beauty. While he worked, a tall white stork, standing upon one leg, watched over him and warned him if anyone approached the door. One night near the end of his labors a slight noise outside warned the stork that someone was lurking there, though Saint Columba was so absorbed in his book that he heard nothing. The stork thrust its bill through a crevice in the door and blinded a young monk who, after an evening of merrymaking with other young men in the monastery, was returning to his cell and was driven by curiosity to peep into the always-locked chamber.

Perhaps the blinding of the monk led to Saint Finnian's discovery of Saint Columba's work; or it may be that Saint Finnian, knowing what an excellent craftsman his guest was, suspected what was going on but allowed the work to continue with the expectation that the book would be his when it was finished. At any rate the wily Saint Finnian kept the secret until the book was complete and then de-

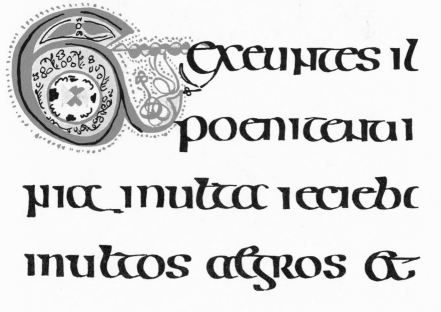

manded that the copy, the handsomest that had ever been
made, be handed over to him.

Saint Columba naturally didn't want to give up the book
over which he had labored so long. A quarrel followed
between the two friends. Finally, not wishing to continue
the unchristian argument, they referred the dispute to the
king of Tara, agreeing to abide by his decision. Each told
his story and then the king gave his famous verdict: "To
every cow its calf; to every book its copy."

Thus Saint Finnian kept at his monastery the famous
Book of Kells, but Saint Columba could not bear the
thought of giving up what he had written with the ap-
proval and in the white light of Heaven, as he believed.
Finally a feud developed between the former friends. Saint
Columba was banished and fled across the sea to the Isle
of Iona in Scotland, where he founded a monastery.

pater ho

Many other beautiful books were produced in Ireland. The semiuncial reached the peak of its perfection there because of the great ability and earnestness of the monks in that isolated country. That isolation, of course, accounts in large part for the national peculiarities of the Irish lettering. While in Rome and the rest of Europe every style of writing, from the Square Capitals and Rustics through all the different variations of uncials and semiuncials, continued and developed side by side until about the seventh century; the Irish scribes used only this alphabet with no outside influences. For years it continued the same with some refinements but no fundamental changes.

We may wonder what was going on in England all this time. Irish missionaries were the first to bring the art of writing to England, but for several centuries nothing distinctive developed in English writing, possibly because their letters were borrowed as full-grown styles from the outside and perhaps also because the influence of continental scribes was so great that the English found no reason for developing a style of their own.

After the seventh century the art of writing remained without any essential change for a long period. There were several reasons. The Dark Ages settled down over Europe with the decay and falling apart of the Roman Empire. As the central government became less powerful, its borders could no longer be defended from the barbarians who kept coming in from the north, the Huns and Visigoths and others who lived by robbery and plunder. Established, peaceful ways of life gave way to a more primitive struggle for existence. Learning and the arts were forgotten in the battle for daily bread.

This decay of the empire that Rome had built up over so many years began as early as the year 410 when the West Goth chief Alaric marched on Rome itself and sacked

and burned the city. A little more than a hundred years
later the Lombards, "longbeards," a nation of wandering

EXPR·MITVR
Visigothic

OROIHA
Anglosaxon

FRATIYM
Spanish

MAYOR
Spanish

ΛΕΝΕΛΣ·
Roman

JUSTIFI
Roman

ꞇaberɥ
French

aucem
English

PROXIM
Continental

DVLCIA
Italian

·AQUA·J
Italian

uade m
Flemish

plunderers, swept down from what is now Germany and conquered all Italy.

In such an unsafe state of society there was only one place where learning could be carried on in peace and quiet, and that was in the monasteries. Isolated on some mountain top such as Monte Cassino in Italy or on some rocky hillside or lonely valley of the Alps, the monks lived in simplicity and poverty hardly worth the trouble of marauders to disturb. It was in such places that the art of writing was preserved. Few changes were made in the forms of the letters at this time, though many "national" hands were developing, some good, some bad. Here are a few of the more important letter forms.

Perhaps the finest writing in all history was done in the quiet of the monasteries. The monks—and sometimes others: refugees, wise men, students, artists, writers—devoted themselves to the making of some of the most beautiful illuminated manuscripts of any time. They worked long hours in lettering and decorating, for they had set themselves the goal of nothing less than perfection in their task. The incentive to excel was kept alive among them by such competitions such as we have already seen between Saint Columba and Saint Finnian.

A little later, however, before the Middle Ages, or Dark Ages, had ended, some new styles did develop that had a marked influence on all writing that followed them and eventually on the printing types that we use today.

Chapter 7

CAROLINE AND GOTHIC LETTERS

Charlemagne, or Charles the Great (Carlo Magnus was his Latin name) became, in the year 768, king of the Franks, a Germanic people living along the river Rhine. Before he died in 814 he had performed so many great deeds that he became the subject of numerous legends.

Among others, the *Song of Roland* tells of the bravery of Charlemagne and his soldiers in their wars against the Saracens or Moors in Spain. His importance in history, however, lies in the fact that he did succeed in bringing some kind of order out of the dark years that fell upon Europe after the Roman Empire had crumbled.

Charlemagne conquered or brought under his authority most of the petty princes and robber barons and local chieftains from western France to the land of the Turks, and from the English Channel to Italy. He was friendly with Pope Leo III who finally crowned him Emperor on Christmas Day in the year 800. His realm, which came to be known as the Holy Roman Empire because it had the blessing of the Church, was not like the Roman Empire whose colonies had been ruled over by governors sent out with Roman legions to enforce their will. It was based

rather on an intricate system of duties and privileges between the princes and barons and lords and their underlings who all paid tribute to the Emperor for his protection and

the guarantee of peace. For the lowest class in this system, the serfs, life was often hard, but for the upper classes and a few privileged ones there was leisure and security.

The feudal system of the middle ages was not ideal from our point of view, but it did permit the development of the arts of civilization. Charlemagne himself was eager to restore learning. He set up schools in various parts of his empire and encouraged artists and men of learning.

In 781 Charlemagne invited to his court a famous English scholar from York named Alcuin, who had been trained in the schools in northern England and had traveled widely. In 796 Alcuin, encouraged by Charlemagne, started a school at the Abbey of Saint Martin's at Tours in

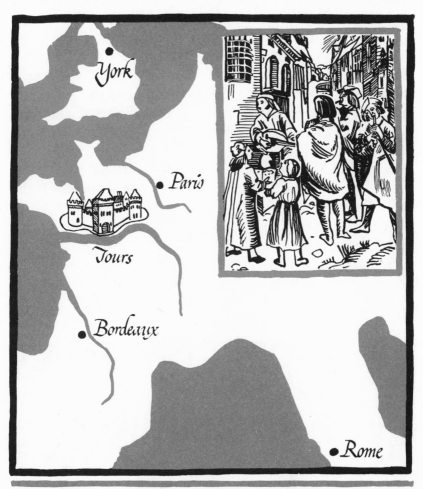

TOURS

the beautiful Loire valley southwest of Paris. There as
abbot he remained until his death in 810. The school he
established at Tours became the most renowned in Europe.
He probably did more than any other man of his day toward the revival of learning.

First of all, Charlemagne gave Alcuin the job of man-
aging the revision and rewriting of all Church literature.
So bad and so various and haphazard had been the European
writing in the troubled years which had marked the break-
up of the old Roman Empire that the Gospels themselves
were in danger of being permanently distorted and lost.
That seemed like a great task, but in addition Charlemagne
ordered a re-editing and rewriting of all the works that
remained of the classical Greek and Roman authors, many
of which had been lost completely or badly copied in the
early Dark Ages.

Alcuin set out first to teach his scribes to write as fine
and readable a hand as possible. Fortunately he had learned
to write the northern type of Anglo-Saxon script, which
was the most beautiful then being written in England. It

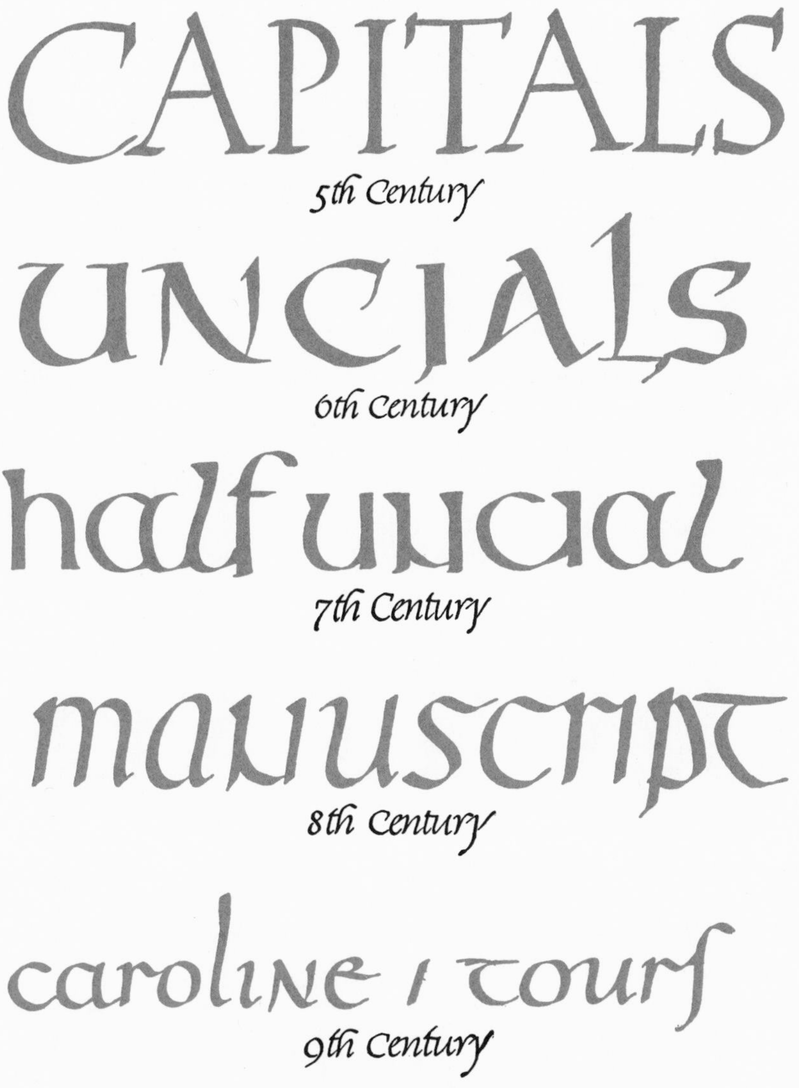

CAPITALS

5th Century

UNCIALS

6th Century

half uncial

7th Century

manuscript

8th Century

caroline / tours

9th Century

was a modification and further development of the semi-uncials of the Irish monks. Based on this form, a new style of writing which Alcuin developed at Tours was to spread throughout Europe and to be the original small letters as we know them today.

The Irish writing itself had finally become complicated with extra frills and decorative strokes and it was no longer so readable as it had been. In the hands of inferior scribes it had become ornate, lacking both handsomeness and usefulness and the beauty of simplicity that the original Roman letters had.

The "Caroline" alphabet (named for Charlemagne) which Alcuin designed, was a true "small-letter" alphabet. The uncials had pointed the way to the small letters, and the semiuncials had gone still further in that direction, but the Caroline letters arrived at forms so closely akin to the letters we use every day in the body of our writing that the resemblance is immediately apparent. Moreover, they were used as we use small letters—as a letter not only smaller than the capital in size but also different in form.

CAPITALS

The sentence now started with a capital and continued with a true minuscule, not just a small capital.

Letters from a ms

Alcuin made a letter so simple in its lines, so free from any finishing frills, that any good scribe could write it well. But above all, it was clear and sharp and *readable*. Some-

et parabsidis intus au

rapina et inmundici

ce mundaprius quod

et parabsidis utfiat

gluttientes. U

i.s scribae etph

times the letters were joined for greater speed in writing, but each was clear and distinct. In fact, the beautiful simplicity of the Caroline letters reminds us of the fine old Roman stone-cut capitals, with which they are ideally suited to harmonize.

When capitals were first used at the heads of paragraphs and sentences, they were thought of as decorations, like the old colored initials, and were frequently made very

DIALOGI ⁏ [I]⁏
Ubjmultjtudohomj
NUM JNSPERATA OCCURRIT
audire ɜ allum defcīmar
aniuircutibuf locuturo
Ubipuellam duodecennemab

fancy. Here is one manuscript that used a line of large capitals and two lines of smaller capitals (uncials, really) before it got started with minuscules—all in one sentence!

Take a closer look at a few individual Caroline letters. It is easy to see how, though so different in character and giving such a different impression on the page, they developed from the original Roman capitals through the forms of the uncials and semiuncials, which, by the way, were still in use in the ninth century. Few of the Caroline letters have a *direct* resemblance to the capitals; they were small and evenly rounded for rapid writing and had strokes extending below the base line of the bodies in *p* and *q*, or above the tops in *b*, *d* and *l*.

We may wonder how the small *b*, for example, came to have the ascending line. At first glance it seems to have little in common with the capital. However, it *is* the capital with the upper lobe omitted! As early as the time of

the Caesars, the capital *B* was often written with the upper bow slightly smaller than the lower. It was still smaller in some of the Rustic letters, and it had entirely disappeared in some of the Roman semiuncials. The *d*, in like manner, grew out of a straightening and lengthening of the slightly extended end line of the rounded *D* of the uncials.

In developing his new alphabet, Alcuin didn't simply modify the writing of his native Northumbria, fine as that was. He had traveled and read widely, and he adopted suggestions he had gained from many different styles. He took the best features from the classical hands of the sixth century and added others from the finest French and Italian writing of his own day. The result was something not different in kind from all alphabets that preceded it but different in character when the letters were put together on the page, more pleasant to the eye and more readable.

Alcuin did much for writing in his few years at Tours, and his influence lived after him. He was the first to systematize the punctuation of manuscripts and the division into sentences and paragraphs.

In the hands of Alcuin's pupils and followers the Caroline small letters continued to improve in gracefulness and finish until they were at their finest in the eleventh and twelfth centuries. The Caroline manuscript hand of the tenth and eleventh centuries later served as one of the models for modern type.

It was natural, however, that its widespread use in many parts of the empire and by many scribes with different training should cause changes in the character of the Caroline alphabet, some slight, some very great indeed. By the end of the Middle Ages a whole new group of national hands had developed just as they had developed at the end of the Roman period.

Only two of these national styles need concern us here. The first, now called "Gothic" or "black-letter," was a written form which evolved in northern Europe and became a distinct style in the twelfth century. In the thirteenth and fourteenth centuries it swept over nearly all of northern Europe and drove out almost all other styles of writing. It is important to us chiefly because the first printers modeled their types upon it.

The name "Gothic" was applied to this alphabet at a much later time when, after the enlightenment of the Renaissance, people began to consider all things of the Middle Ages as rude and barbaric like the Goths who invaded Rome in the fifth century. Hence it was a term of contempt and scorn. Even the beautiful architecture of the Medieval cathedrals, such as the one at Antwerp pictured here, was dubbed Gothic by people who thought nothing was beautiful or civilized except the round and balanced forms of classical times.

Round Gothic

Pointed Gothic

Pointed condensed got

Various influences lead to the development of this Gothic. For some reason—some say it was a shortage of parchment which forced the scribes to crowd as much as possible on a page—a tendency was growing to make letters very narrow and angular. Or it may be that these stiff, narrow, angular letters were at first the coarse and awkward writing of scribes who couldn't handle the graceful curves of the Caroline alphabet and so got into the habit of making a series of parallel strokes, joining them where it was necessary to complete the letters.

Gradually the perpendicular strokes became very fat and the others very thin, practically hairlines. This was the

extreme condensed Gothic. There was also a round Gothic. Because of the heavy, thick lines, however, they all looked very black on the page—hence the term "black-letter."

As a break in the monotony of the exceptionally rigid, stiff, angular letters of the condensed Gothic—which came to be little more than row upon row of exactly similar thick perpendicular lines crowded together and joined by almost invisibly thin oblique hairlines—new Gothic capitals came into use, some of which tended to roundness and all of which were elaborately decorated and full of flourishes. Though they didn't always harmonize with the small letters, they did make the manuscript page more interesting, especially when they were done in color. We still use some of these Gothic capitals designed in the Middle Ages (and modern ones in their spirit) for initial letters. There was no set form for the Gothic capital; the artist or writer had almost perfect freedom to design any shape that struck his fancy so long as it had some resemblance to the letter and plenty of bold curves and angles. Some of them were modeled on the forms of the old uncials.

The Gothic "black letter" became particularly popular in Germany and the Low Countries (Holland and Belgium). A manuscript hand developed there which was happily not too fat nor too thin, and which had more variety and interest than the extreme forms. When the first printers began their work in Germany, it was this letter they copied for their types. The strange thing is that, within a hundred years after printing began, the Gothic had disappeared almost everywhere except in Germany where it has lasted both in handwriting and in printing to our own day.

Some Gothic writing was very handsome when written by skilled scribes, and many beautiful manuscripts were made with these letters in the thirteenth and fourteenth centuries. They are not readable for us, of course, for we are used to the round and open letters of the Caroline style, and the blackness of the page is strange to us.

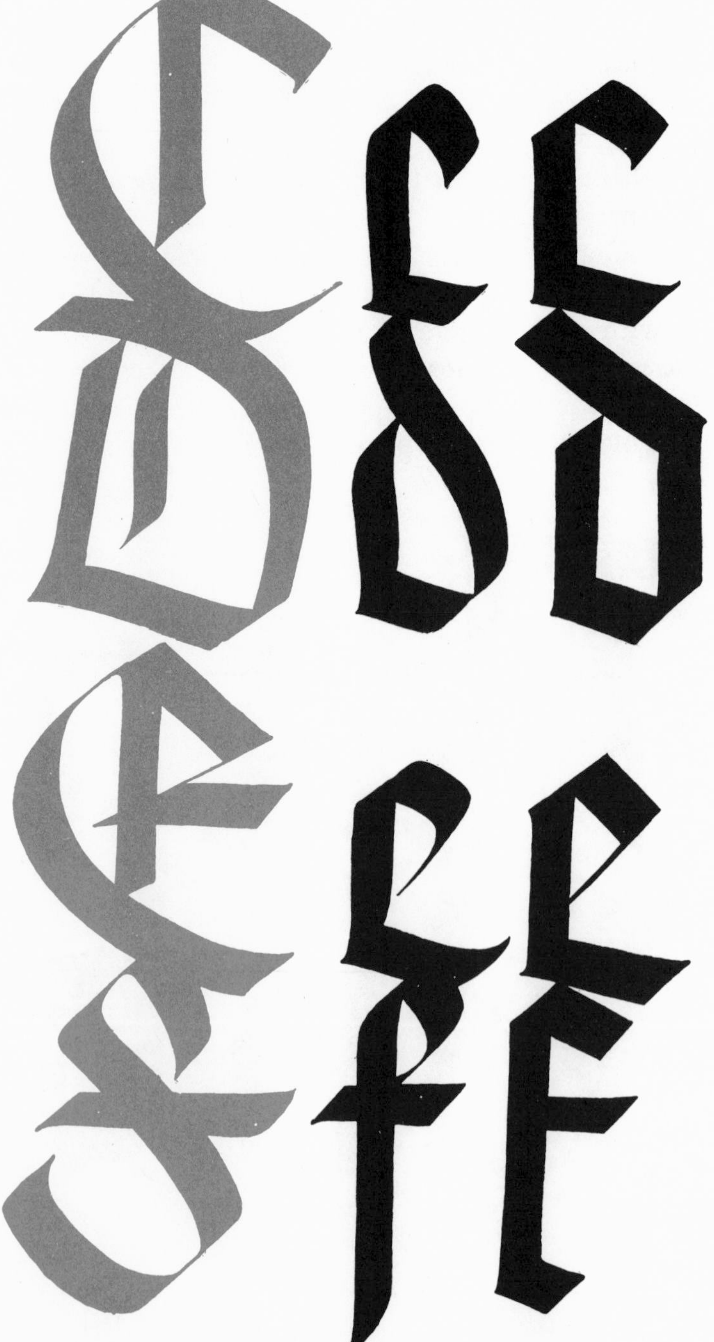

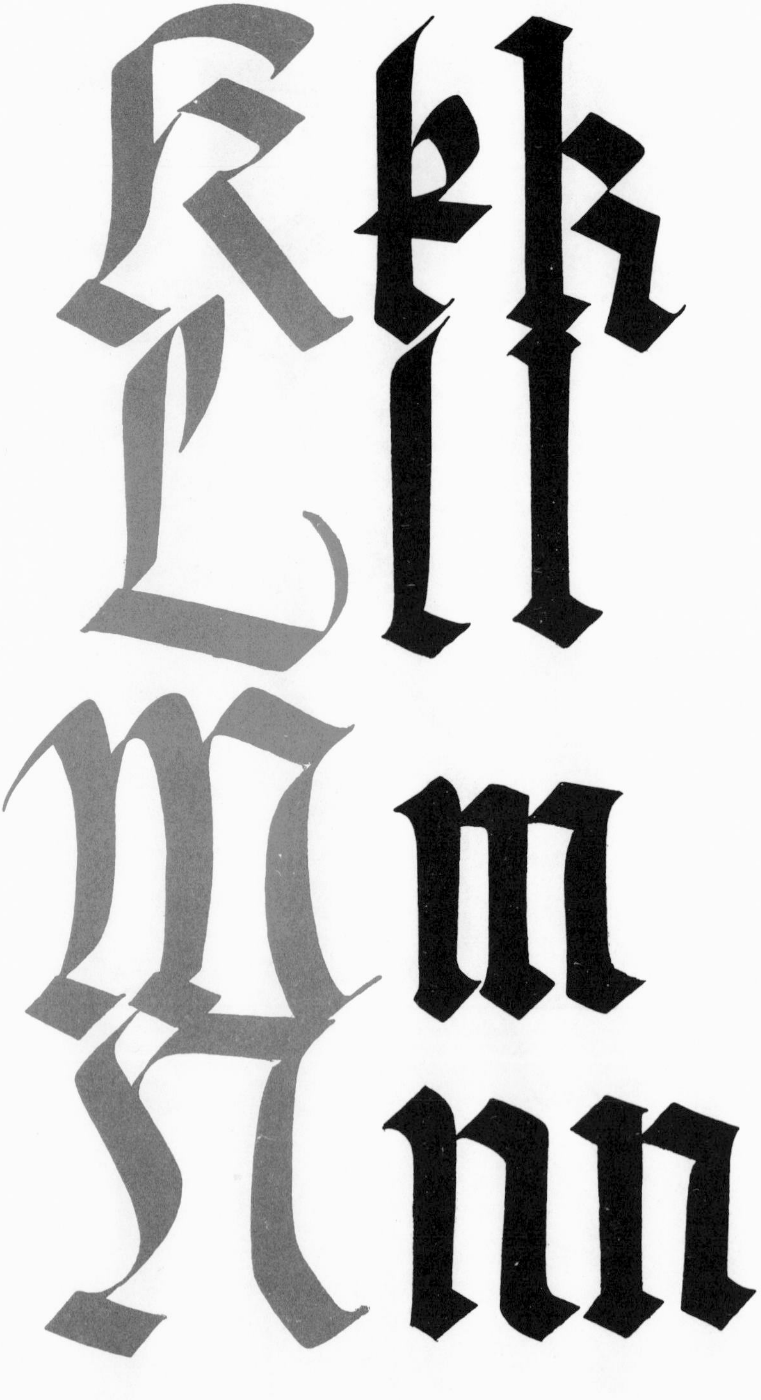

Kk Ll Kk Ll

Mm Nn Mm Nn

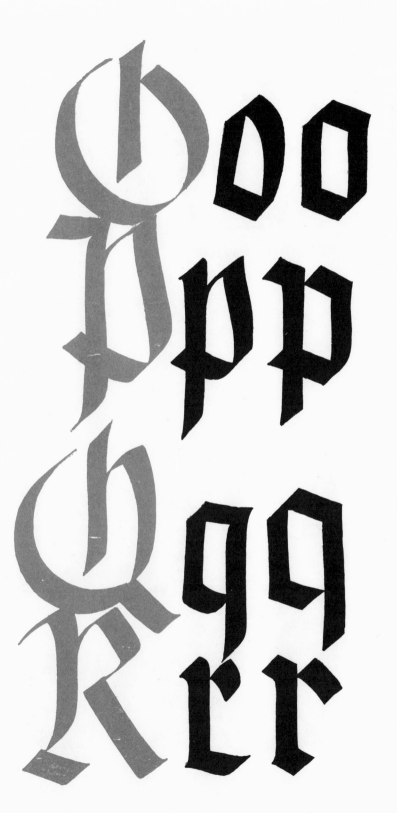

Oo Opp
Oh Gqq
QRr Rrr

S sſ ſ

T tt tt

U luu uu

V vv vv

One of the reasons for the final abandonment of the Gothic may be seen in the development, in the tenth century, of one of the other national hands, the so-called Italian round hand or "cursive" based on earlier Roman

Tenth century ital-

letters. One sixteenth-century form of this hand, a slanted letter, became very popular throughout Europe after the introduction of printing, principally because it was made into a type by the Venetian printer Aldus. In France it was called "italic," the name by which it is still known to French and English readers. Another form of the Italian hand, straightened, and a perfected Caroline alphabet finally all but displaced the Gothic.

Let us look back now for a moment before we leave the ages during which the letter forms were controlled by the pen. The diagram will help us to do that. The Phoenician characters, like the same Egyptian hieroglyphics and the hieratic script, were written with a reed pen on papyrus. The stiff and sharp-angled letters of the Greek alphabet owe their first forms to the use of a pointed stylus on wax tablets, but they too developed more curves and grace when later they came to be written with a pen on parchment. We also have seen that, though the first Roman capitals were carved on stone, it was really the drawing which preceded the work of the stonecutter that determined their form. The handsome curves of the Trajan capitals, the varying widths of the lines, was the work of an instrument which, if not a pen, had much the same effect. From then on, from the written Square capitals and the Rustics down through all the variations of the uncials and semiuncials, the finest Caroline hands of the Middle Ages, and all of the Blackletters, the pen determined shape and gave final character to the forms of letters.

1400 BC	ΔΨ٦ᗡ Ⅎ Ⴙ ⅄ ⲙ
800 BC	ΑΒΓΔΕΗΚ
100 BC	ABCDEHKM
300 AD	ABCDEHKM
800	abcdehkm
900	Abcdefghikm
1100	abcdefghikm
1200	abcdefghiklmno
1400	abcdefghiklm

Now we enter a period when letters will be controlled by working metal type and by printing practices.

Chapter 8

THE INVENTION OF TYPE

Johann Gutenberg is a name with which most of us are familiar. If we were asked what he was famous for, we should probably reply: "He was the man who invented printing." But like so many accepted statements, this is not exactly true.

Gutenberg family seal

Before we look more closely at what this very interesting though little-known man actually had to do with printing,

186

let us turn back to several important events and discoveries before his day. On the other side of the world in China, in A.D. 105, at a time when the Romans were just extending their conquests among the wild Celtic tribes of Britain, a government official by the name of Tsai Lun reported to the emperor a very interesting process which he had either invented himself or found others using. As he described it, bark from trees, hemp and rags were cut up, pounded into a pulp, mixed with water and placed in a vessel for cooking. The "mush" was poured onto screens of closely spaced bamboo strips; and, when the water drained off, the remainder dried into thin sheets very like our modern paper.

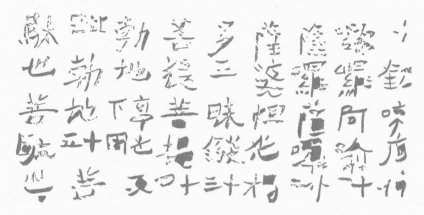

The Chinese discovered about this time, too, a way to repeat designs and pictures on this new paper. First they carved the design on a block of wood, then they "inked" it and pressed it on the paper, or the paper on it. This was real printing, as far as the principle is concerned, and the first of the kind that we know of, although even before that the Babylonians and other Near Eastern peoples had known how to make impressions on wax and other surfaces with carved seals and rings. The Chinese, however, took the next logical step, and we know scrolls were being printed in Chinese characters from wood blocks by the seventh century. Printing from separate "types" carved from wood followed; it may have been as early as the eleventh century, but certainly by the fourteenth. A book printed in 1337 in Korea (then a part of China) from movable blocks is now in the British Museum. Thus the credit for the invention of printing really belongs to the Chinese. This art might have developed further and more rapidly if it hadn't been impractical to make movable type for an alphabet of 6,000 characters for everyday use and a possible 40,000 for the complete written language!

It seems strange that Marco Polo, the great Venetian adventurer who in the thirteenth century spent seventeen years in the realm of Cathay, as China was then called, should have had nothing to say in his famous *Travels* about such an important invention. He visited all the provinces of China and paid his respects to the emperor, Kublai Khan, near Peking. He had his eyes open for many strange customs; but apparently he did not see, or at least he did not bring back to Europe any information concerning, a printing process. All that was learned about printing in Europe in the fifteenth century was worked out independently, without knowledge of what the Chinese had done. European printing type was a separate invention, and it went far beyond anything that had been done before anywhere.

The making of paper, however, did find its way to Europe from the Orient by a long and roundabout way. In the eigth century the Arabs conquered Samarkand, a remote land in central Asia, and among their prisoners were two Chinese paper makers. By the twelfth century those Arabs, known as Moors, carried the art of paper-making to Spain, and later in that century it was known in France. But much of the early printing in Europe was done on parchment, for paper was not thought strong enough.

Soon, however, the rapid growth of printing forced the use of paper. There was not enough parchment to feed the printing presses, each of which could turn out a hundred sheets while a scribe was copying three or four. More and more attention began to be given to the manufacture of paper. Queen Elizabeth in 1589 gave, as a special privilege, a kind of monopoly to her jeweler, Sir John Spilman. He was authorized to make for ten years "all manner of paper from rags, old fishing nets, odds and ends of used parchments."

Now we come back to Johann Gutenberg. We know so little about him that many people have been tempted to

complete the story of his life and work with some pretty far-flung guesses based on very slight evidence and much speculation. We shall try here to stick to known facts as far as possible. Beyond that each may use his own imagination as he chooses.

He was born about 1397 in the old town of Mainz on the upper Rhine in Germany. We know that Johann's parents while he was still quite young went to live in Strasbourg farther up the Rhine in the province of Alsace. His father's name was Friele zum Gensfleisch. Possibly Johann took the name of Gutenberg, his mother's birthplace, because he preferred to go through life with a name that meant "Good Mountain" rather than with one that meant "Goose Flesh."

He was living in Strasbourg in 1434, but he also had some relations with people in Mainz, for in that year he seized the town clerk of Mainz for a debt due him. From this time on we always hear of him in connection with lawsuits, either that he is bringing against others or that

they are bringing against him. This doesn't mean necessarily that he was more quarrelsome than other people or
that he was dishonest in money matters. It may mean only
that the peculiar business he was engaged in demanded
legal action occasionally to straighten out the money ar-
rangements. At any rate, if it hadn't been for the law suits,
we should have practically no Gutenberg records at all.

The first of these groups of court records is called the
"Strasbourg Documents of 1439." They are the records

of a trial connected with the dissolving of a partnership
into which Gutenberg had entered some years before for
the purpose of perfecting some kind of tools for a craft
which is not mentioned by name but which might well
have been printing. It is tantalizing that not one of the
sixteen witnesses whose testimony was preserved actually
named or described the business that the partners were
engaged in. It is because undoubtedly Gutenberg was bor-
rowing money a few years later to carry on experiments in

what appears to have been printing that we suppose he was
working at the same problem back in 1435 or 1436. Before
the documents of the trial had been copied or thoroughly
examined, they were destroyed when the Germans marched
into Strasbourg in the Franco-Prussian War of 1870.

Gutenberg was still in Strasbourg in 1441 and 1442.
Then he vanished until about 1448 when he had evidently
returned to Mainz, the town of his birth. There in 1450
he seems to have been in partnership with Johann Fust, a
goldsmith, who furnished him with money for "tools" and
experiments. These were connected with the devising and
casting of movable type for printing.

If we could only look in on him during the next five
years there in his shop in Mainz! When we see him again
in 1455 he is once more in trouble. In that year the goldsmith Fust sued him to recover his money or the "tools."
Gutenberg, his work not being a financial success, lost the
equipment. Fust and his son-in-law, Peter Schoeffer,
started a printing business in Mainz about that time. It is
ironical that they probably used the very tools that Gutenberg had perfected. The new partners printed the first
dated book from movable type, a psalter in Latin, in 1457,
and they continued printing for a number of years.

There is some evidence, however, that Gutenberg himself did some printing with these tools before he had to
give them up. A papal indulgence printed at Mainz in
1454 may well have been his work, and the great 42-line
Bible completed in 1456, though it is not signed or dated,
was probably set from the movable type that he invented,
whether it was actually printed by Gutenberg or by Fust
and Schoeffer. This Bible, commonly believed to be the
first book printed from movable metal type cast in molds,
is generally referred to as the Gutenberg Bible, though it

obsedit me. Foderut manus meas
et pedes meos: dinumerauerut oia
ossa mea. Ipsi vero cosiderauerunt
et inspererut me: diuiserunt sibi vesti
menta mea: et sup veste mea miserut
sortem. Tu aut due ne elongaueris
auxiliu tuu: ad defensione mea ospice.
Erue a framea deus anima mea: et
de manu canis vnica mea. Sal
ua me er ore leonis: et a cornibz vni
corniu humilitate mea. Narrabo no
men tuu fratribz meis: in medio eccle
sie laudabo te. Qui timetis dum lau
date eu: vniusu seme iacob glorifica
te eu. Timeat eu oie seme israhel:
quonia no spreuit neqz despexit depre
catione pauperis. Nec auertit faciem
sua a me: et cu clamare ad eu exaudi
uit me. Aput te laus mea in ecclesia
magna: vota mea reddam in cospectu
timetiu eu. Edent pauperes et satura
butur: et laudabut dum qui requirut
eu: viuet corda eoz in seclm seculi. Re
miniscentur et conuertentur ad dum:
vniusi fines terre. Et adorabunt in
cospectu ei9: vniuse familie gentium.
Quonia dui est regnu: et ipse dnabi
tur gentiu. Manducauerut et adora
uerut omnes pingues terre: in cospectu
eius cadet omnes qui descendut in ter
ram. Et anima mea illi viuet: et se
men meu seruiet ipi. Annunciabitur
dno generatio ventura: et annuncia
bunt celi iusticia ei9 ipso qui nascetur
quem fecit dominus. psalm9 dauid XXII
Dominus regit me et nichil michi
deerit: in loco pascue ibi me col
locauit. Super aqua refectionis edu
rauit me: anima mea couertit. De
duxit me super semitas iusticie: ppter
nomen suu. Nam et si ambulauero
in medio vmbre mortis non timebo

mala: quonia tu mecum es. Virga
tua et baculus tuus: ipa me cosolata
sunt. Parasti in cospectu meo mesa:
aduersus eos qui tribulat me. Impin
guasti in oleo caput meu: et calix me
us inebrias quam pclarus est. Et mi
sericordia tua subsequetur me: oibz
diebz vite mee. Et ut inhabitem i do
mo domini: in longitudine dierum.
psalm9 dauid in pma sabbati. XXIII
Domini est terra et plenitudo ei9:
orbis terrau et vniuersi qui habi
tant in eo. Quia ipse sup maria fun
dauit eu: et super flumina preparauit
eu. Quis ascendit i montem dni: aut
quis stabit in loco sancto ei9. Inno
cens manibz et mudo corde: qui non
accepit in vano anima sua: nec iura
uit in dolo proximo suo. Hic accipi
et benedictione a dno: et misericordiam
a deo salutari suo. Hec est generatio
querentiu eu: querentiu facie dei iacob.
Attollite portas principes vestras
et eleuamini porte eternales: et introi
bit rex glorie. Quis e iste rex glorie?
dns fortis et potens: domin9 potes in
prelio. Attollite portas principes ve
stras et eleuamini porte eternales: et
introibit rex glorie. Quis est iste rex
glorie? dominus virtutum ipse est
rex glorie. In fine psalm9 dauid XXIIII
Ad te dne leuaui anima mea: de
us me9 i te cofido no erubesca. Neqz
irrideant me inimici mei: etenim vni
uersi qui sustinet te no confundentur.
Confundantur omnes iniqua agen
tes: super vacue. Vias tuas domine
demostra michi: et semitas tuas edo
ce me. Dirige me in veritate tua et do
ce me: quia tu es deus saluator me9:
et te sustinui tota die. Reminiscere
miseracionu tuarum dne: et misedia2

is often called also the Mazarin Bible because the first copy
to draw the attention of people interested in early printed
books was in the library of Cardinal Mazarin in Paris.
The large pages had two columns of forty-two lines each in
a block letter about twice as large as our ordinary book type.

Gutenberg was still in Mainz in 1457, and it is likely
that he got other financial backing and continued printing
until his death in 1468. No books bear his name and no
genuine portrait of him is known. Pictures and statues of
him are all drawn from imagination (including, naturally,
the one we have here!)

With so little known of the man, why has he been so
celebrated? The best answer is that when curiosity was
first aroused about the origins of printing he seemed to have
the most logical claim to its invention. Hearsay accounts
of those who had gone to Mainz from all over Europe to
learn the new art named him the inventor of the process
of printing from movable type. The very haziness of the
facts of his life began to settle like a halo around his head.
At any rate, it can be said with reasonable certainty that
Gutenberg helped to perfect a method for printing from
movable metal type and that he had a great deal to do
with the first actual use of these types.

That perhaps is enough to justify his fame, even if no
printing can be pointed to as unquestionably his work.

The development of the technique perfected by Gutenberg, and the conditions leading to it, extend over a long
period. In the first place, with the Renaissance in Europe
(the "rebirth" of interest in the old literature and philosophy of Greece and Rome and a general reawakening of
curiosity about many things outside of the church literature) there came such a demand for books that all the
scribes copying at top speed could no longer supply them.
More people were learning to read than ever before.

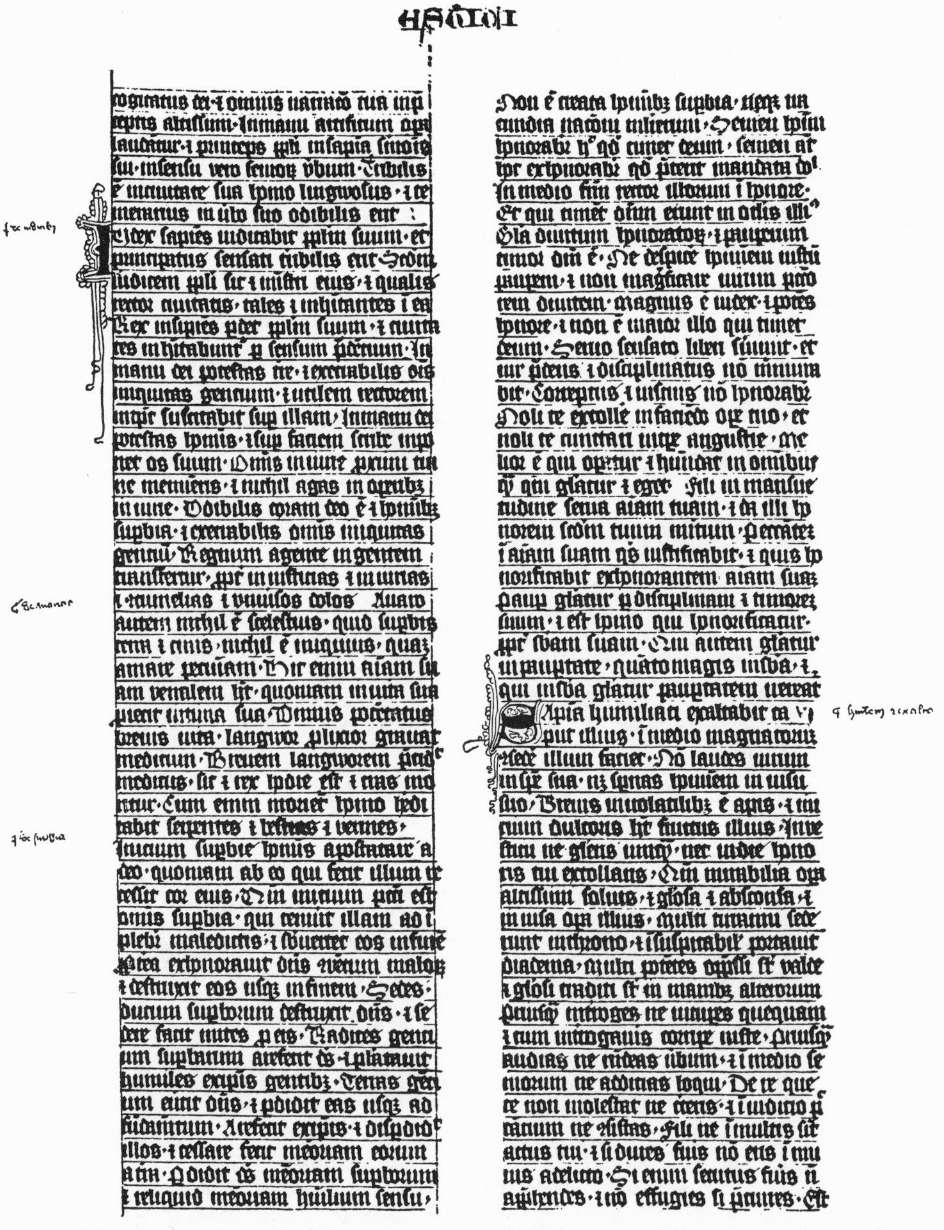

Manuscript Bible page, model for early printed work

Repofitio quid eft: Partora
tionis que p pofita aliis par
tibus oratois fignification
eai aut complet.

From early block books

Wealthy middle class tradesmen sent their sons to schools and to the universities of Oxford or Cambridge, or to Paris or Bologna. Those sons wanted to know more about the new ideas which were coming from Italy. They wanted to read not only the Scriptures but also the works of the Latin poets Virgil and Ovid and those new Italian writers who were producing such interesting love poems and stories —Dante, Petrarch, Boccaccio. They even wanted to read such things as Chaucer's *Canterbury Tales*, written in the language of the day instead of in Latin.

Much earlier, pictures and letters had been cut in wood blocks and printed in manuscript books. A few years before Gutenberg began his experiments, attempts were even being made to reproduce whole books without the great labor of handwriting. At this time block books such as the Chinese had made were being printed in some numbers from carved wood blocks, the pictures and the letters being cut in one solid piece of wood. These blocks were tedious to cut and, of course, their use was limited to a particular text. Once that text had been printed, the blocks of the pages were of no further value.

The next logical step was to cut the alphabet in *individual letters* so that it could be used for any text by simply combining the letters. These carved letters came very close to *type*.

A piece of type is a bar, on one end of which projects the shape of a letter in reverse. When this reverse letter is wet with ink and pressed against a sheet of paper, it leaves the image of the letter right side up and as it should be. The letters are arranged in words and lines; and, when as many copies have been made as are wanted, the type can be returned to the cases and used again to print other texts. This looks like a simple idea, but what problems the inventor had to solve before it could be used successfully!

First, he had to find a way of making each piece of type exactly like every other—of making it *controlled in size.* It had to be exactly rectangular so it would fit snugly with

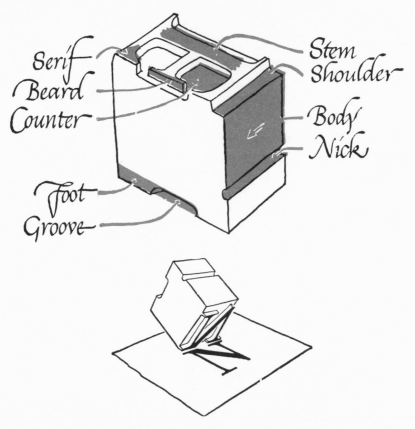

its neighbors in the line, and absolutely right in height to a hair's breadth or the inked surface of the type would not print evenly or true.

Second, for economy and speed he had to find a way to make many pieces of type, each identical with the others, from a master pattern. He had to devise a means of *casting* the type in a mold from metal soft enough to be easily melted and hard enough to bear the pressure of the printing.

Third, there had to be a method of holding the type

together solidly in one block the size of a page and of pressing the paper evenly upon it after it was inked. There had to be a *press*.

We do not know exactly how Gutenberg, or perhaps Gutenberg and others, solved the three basic problems and perfected the printing process. Between the earliest known activity in the subject and the first really successful book printed from type there was a span of about twenty years.

If we are realistic in our speculations and guesses, we shall assume that someone before Gutenberg probably solved parts of all the problems—probably arrived at the very threshold of success. That is usually true of most great inventions. How many before him almost succeeded we do not know, nor how far they got, nor how much he borrowed from their work, nor who they were. All that is a mystery which is not likely ever to be solved.

But looking back from the accomplished result, let us follow Gutenberg in imagination as he puttered about his shop during those eventful four or five years when we may suppose he was perfecting the great invention.

First he tried one metal and then another, until finally he struck upon a combination of them, an alloy, that would melt at a fairly low temperature and then cool and solidify without shrinking. We may see from the drawing on page 200 why a metal that shrinks in cooling could not be used. The pieces of type would never fit together tightly. That was what he had been looking for; now he could make types that would not differ a fraction of an inch one from another. This combination of metals, lead mixed with antimony and tin, is exactly like the one we use today for printers' type. No one in the whole five hundred years of printing history has found a better one. Gutenberg had solved the first problem. The dimensions of the type could be controlled.

Next he had to construct a device that would make this

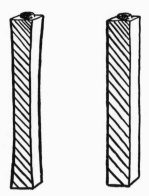

type, one that could be used over and over again. Casting
had been done before, for coins and the like, but the mold
had to be destroyed to get the coin out. There was no great
likelihood that any two coins would be *exactly* alike as we
have seen that type must be to print accurately.

Gutenberg's solution was probably like this. He made
four pieces of wood or metal which locked together accurately leaving an open space between them the size and
shape he wanted the body of his type to be. At the bottom
of this open space, closing it off, he fitted a matrix—a

master form which had the letter cut into it. When the
melted metal was poured into the form, it filled the whole
space including every line and curve of the letter as it was
cut in the matrix. Then the mold was opened and a little
type bar removed, with the raised-up letter on its end, in

reverse, ready for inking. The mold could be put together again for making the next letter or more of the same one.

Designing the matrix itself was not difficult. A hard steel punch was cut the size and shape of the desired letter and driven into the plate a measured distance. This formed the depression into which the lead flowed. Such a process had long been in use by medieval jewelers and

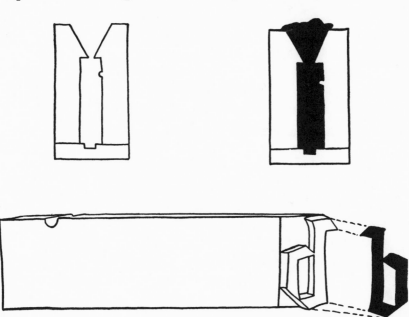

engravers. Gutenberg had only to borrow the principle and use it with his new kind of mold that could be taken apart and used again, and his second problem, that of casting the type, was solved.

Inking and printing had been done before, but not with movable metal type. The ink offered several minor problems. Early Chinese printers had used something like our water colors of today. The liquid soaked into the wood of the block and then the paper was applied to it. However,

Counter-punch, the shape of the inside of the letter

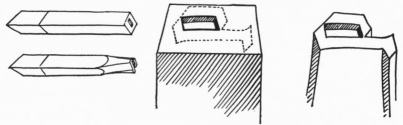

Punch, made by driving the counter-punch into the end of the punch, then filing around it to form the letter.

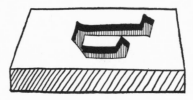

It is then driven into the matrix and the matrix cast in lead (see drawing on page 201).

with metal type a sticky ink had to be used, one which would stay on the surface of the type and yet could be transferred to the parchment or paper when pressure was applied. Gutenberg found the solution in the paints that artists used. The ingredients—linseed oil, varnish, and pigment—are the same now as they were when Gutenberg first experimented with them.

The press for printing came almost ready made, too, for the earliest printer. Presses for various purposes which

worked on the principle of the screw had long been used.
All Gutenberg had to do was to arrange the bed for the
type at a convenient height, make it slide easily under the
press for printing and out for inking; fix the screw so only
a short turn would bring the pressure down or release it;

and add a device for holding the parchment or paper in
position. The third problem was solved, and with its solution the first printing from movable type could be done
successfully. The excellence of the books printed shortly
after Gutenberg is assumed to have been experimenting
with printing shows how well all the major problems were
solved at that time. The speed and accuracy of printing
machines have increased incredibly since then, but we have
few more beautiful books than the famous Gutenberg
Bible, printed about 1456 by methods as simple as those we
have just described.

Various other persons have been held to be the inventor
of movable type. As we have mentioned, others may have
worked on the process before Gutenberg and even solved
some of the problems. There was, for instance, one Lourens

Fifteenth-century print shop

Janszoon Coster (or Koster), a Dutchman living in Haar-
lem, who is put forth by some as the real inventor of printing from movable type. All the evidence, however, comes
from an account of his work written more than a hundred
years after his death in 1440. There have been discovered,

it is true, inside the bindings of a number of old books, some scraps of parchment with letters on them which were printed from movable type before Gutenberg's time. Those who claim that Coster was the real inventor point to these and say they were *probably* Coster's work.

Perhaps it is true, but we do not know. The question is, how successful was he in his work? Did he solve all the

problems of type-making and printing as well as Gutenberg did? He may have been on the verge of success, as perhaps many others had been, and then something went wrong: his metal was too hard or too soft or not durable enough, or it shrank in the mold, or his press was not efficient. It seems likely that he missed somewhere, or his work would have been copied by others in Holland.

Only one other rival claim to the invention need be mentioned and that only briefly, for there seems to be no real evidence to support it. A seventeenth-century Italian historian, perhaps eager to claim the honor for one of his countrymen, contended that a certain Pamfilo Castaldi preceded Gutenberg in printing from movable type. But all that is known about him for certain is that he was the first printer in Milan.

This new method of making books was slow in getting under way for a few years, and then it spread very rapidly.

At first, the appeal of manuscript books to the reading
public was so great that the printer tried to imitate the
work of the scribes, not only in the letter forms themselves,
but in the style and manner in which they were used.
Scribes or artists were hired to add by hand big initial letters, for which space had been left, and sometimes decora-

atus vir qui non
abijt in oſilio impiorꝫ:
et in via peccatoꝛu non
ſtetit: ꞇ in cathedra peſti
lentie non ſedit,   ed
in lege domini volutas
eius: ꞇ in lege eius meditabitur die ac no-
de,   t erit tanꝗʒ lignu quod platatu eſt
ſecus decurſus aꝗ: qd fructu ſuu dabit in
tpe ſuo   t foliu ei⁹ no defluet: ꞇ oia qcuꝗʒ
faciet ꝑſperabut,   o ſic impij no ſic: ſed
tanꝗʒ puluis que ꝓiat ventus a facie terre.
deo non reſurgut impij in iudicio neꝗʒ
pcoꝛes in coſilio iuſtoꝛ,   m nouit dms
via iuſtoꝛ et iter impioꝛ peribit,   ſia

An early book page, set and printed
and ready for completion by a scribe.

Eatus vir qui non
abiit in cōsilio impiorū:
et in via peccatorū non
stetit: ⁊ in cathedra pesti-
lentie non sedit, Sed
in lege dominū volutas
eius: ⁊ in lege eius meditabitur die ac no-
cte, Et erit tanqʒ lignū quod plātatū est
sems decursus aqaͥ: qd fructū suū dabit in
tpͤ suo Et foliū ei⁹ nō defluet: ⁊ oīa qͣcūqʒ
faciet prͤsperabūt, Nō sic impiī nō sic: sed
tanqʒ puluis quē proͥcͥt ventus a facie terre.
Ideo non resurgūt impiī in iudicio neqʒ
pcͤcͤores in cōsilio iustorͣ, Qm nouit dn̄s
via iustorͣ et iter impiorͣ peribit, Gͤla Pͤs

The same page after the scribe had completed the
illuminations, musical score, and rubrication.

tions and illustrations in the margins. Of course, as far as
the beauty of books was concerned, the first printer had a
serious rival in the best of the scribes, for he could hardly
hope to equal with metal types and often makeshift and
crude presses the fine hand work of the skilled artists who
made the books of the Middle Ages.

But finally speed and quantity and inexpensiveness won.
And as the demand for books increased the process of

From the First FLINT WEAPON *to the First* CAVE DRAWING *(2)0,000 Years)*

From CAVE DRAWINGS *to* HIEROGLYPHICS *(15,000 Years)*

HIEROGLYPHICS *to* ROMAN LETTERS
(5000 Years)

ROMAN LETTERS *to the In-
vention of Printing
(1500 Years)*

*Time required for the
spread of Printing
throughout Europe
(35 Years)*

making them had to be speeded up. The printer did more
and more of the book in type and depended less and less

upon hand work for the finishing. It was not too difficult to design types which imitated the scribe's work. Finally the more florid decorations disappeared and were largely replaced by simple initials or capital letters at the heads of chapters and paragraphs.

Before long the books printed by the group of pioneers in Mainz were known throughout Europe, and artisans came there to learn the trade. Among the first and most famous of these was Nicolas Jenson, master of the mint (official maker of coins) at Tours under the French king Charles VII. And here is pretty strong evidence which we have not mentioned before that Gutenberg's reputation soon got abroad among his contemporaries as the inventor of the new printing method. A French court record says: "On the 3rd of October, 1458, the king having found that Sieur Gutenberg, Knight, living at Mayence [the French spelling of Mainz], Germany, a man dexterous in engraving and in making letter punches, had brought to light an invention for printing with metal characters," sent Jenson to Mainz with instructions to inform himself secretly of the invention. The mint master was the right person to send, for he already knew something of the processes of engraving or cutting designs, of printing, stamping, and casting in connection with his work in making coins.

Many others came to learn the new art. Mainz became the center of bookmaking and remained so until the sack of the city in 1462 by the conquering army of Adolphus of Nassau scattered the printers. Then many who had learned their trade in Germany set up their equipment in other lands, at first in Italy where in the full flood of the Renaissance there were many wealthy patrons of the arts to encourage them. Within thirty-five years printing had spread to every country in Europe.

The Spread of PRINTING

1483

1482

1476

1473   1454

1473

1470

1468

1487

1474

1465

Germany	1454	Austria Hungary	1473
Italy	1465	Spain	1474
Switzerland	1468	England	1476
France	1470	Denmark	1482
Holland	1473	Sweden	1483
Belgium	1473	Portugal	1487

The difficulties of the wandering printer were many. Carrying on his own or a donkey's back a few tools, his matrices, and perhaps a few fonts (complete sets of the same style or size of type), he settled down and opened a shop in some strange town where perhaps even the language was new to him. There he had to build a press and all new equipment completely alone.

His new clients spoke another language and had other tastes in letters than those of his native city. So he set to work, first learning the language of his new neighbors, then designing a new type by copying carefully some popular manuscript hand of the vicinity or some favored scribe's lettering, next cutting his punches, stamping matrices, casting his type, and printing. He bound his own books and he sold them too.

Since different styles of letters were demanded for different purposes, the early printer had to stock at least three

Roman Let

different faces. Roman letters were generally preferred for

Black Letter

the classics, Gothic types for other books in Latin, and

Familiar Let

adaptations of local manuscript hands for books in the language of the country in which the printer worked. Thus a great variety of type styles grew up where we might have expected only a few at the beginning of this youngest of the arts. By about 1480, however, printers were using only a relatively few standard styles that had become well established in certain popular or well-known books. They ceased copying all the different handwritings of the time. Styles became fairly definitely fixed.

That, of course, is why the invention of printing has had such a tremendous influence on the development of our letter forms. The tool governs the form again. Henceforth there no longer will be a feel of the pen in our alphabet.

Great Britain

In the fifteenth century our letters changed from free-flowing written symbols to mechanical uniform cast-metal characters. The *forms* of letters became definitely fixed.

Great Britain

After this time they did not show any major changes comparable to the ones that took place when the scribe was master and the varied traditions of the manuscript prevailed. We may see this best perhaps if we compare the changes that have taken place in printed books in the last four hundred years with the changes that took place in letter forms in the four hundred years before printing! We can read easily a book printed in Shakespeare's day, but the handwriting of the thirteenth century is markedly different from our own!

Changes of a very important kind have come about in our letters, however, since the invention of type. The story of the development of our alphabet during five hundred years of printing from type is the final chapter in its history.

Chapter 9

PRINTING AND THE ALPHABET

When printing was first developed in Germany, the letters used, as we have seen, were black letters—the only letter style in general use there at the time. But as wandering printers carried the art to other lands, many other letter styles were cast and became popular before the end of the fifteenth century. Some of these reflected only passing fads or fashions or local tastes, but a few were so simple and fine and legible that they finally triumphed over the Gothic black letter and had a permanent effect upon later printed letter forms. An early one of these was the roman type, which was not a new style at all but only a slight modification of the Caroline hand as it was then written in Italy.

Shortly after 1462, two German printers, Conrad Sweynheim and Arnold Pannartz, set up their presses and began printing at the Benedictine monastery at Subiaco, near Rome. The Renaissance had by then spread throughout Europe. But the home of the new birth of learning was Italy where it had started more than a century before. There were many patrons of printing both in and out of the church to encourage the makers of books.

After a few experiments with types that would suit the tastes of their Italian customers, who had never taken

Domine omnipotens

Pointed English Gothic

Domine omnipotens

Round French Gothic

Domine omnipotens

French Familiar

Forma plenissime
Remittendo tibi

German Gothic (pointed and round)

In theologia

Kroberger, 1480

Ipsum autem

Rusch (first German Roman)

Sarmaria Asiatica

Holle (transitional Roman)

Romā deporta

Sweynheim and Pannartz, 1465

nos in libro

Italian Roman

vizi domini guido

French Gothic

Et en sa touchoit

Dutch Familiar

Lotiene mas los hy

Spanish Round Gothic

For Salamon saith

English Text

E xpectes eadem a summo,

Aldus Italic, 1501

kindly to the sharp angular Gothic letters imported from the north, Sweynheim designed, cut, and cast a roman type; with it his partner Pannartz printed a beautiful large book in 1464 or 1465—the first dated book (from type) published in Italy. The letters that were cut for this book were classic in general form, but they had a German flavor. They were Roman in style but Gothic in character. Sweynheim

de ſumo &

seems to have been trying to imitate the graceful rounded roman pen letters with their gradual curves, delicate serifs bracketed into the stems, and other roman characteristics. But, perhaps because he was so greatly influenced by the northern style of writing, he gave the letters a little black-letter character. If we enlarge them we see that they have

de ſumo &   de ſumo &

a sharpness at the turns, especially at the tops, and that there are no real serifs but only a little broadening at the ends of the upright strokes. Yet this was the father of all our roman types. Three years later these pioneer printers were using a type that had lost most of its Gothic character. It is so much like our modern types that except for the long (S) we would scarcely know the difference.

Venice soon became the center of Italian printing. Some of the finest printing of all time was done there before

the end of the fifteenth century. The first seems to have
been the work of Johann da Spira, another German printer,
who had settled there as early as 1469. In that year he
printed the *Letters of Cicero* and a volume of the Latin
writer Tacitus in a type that he had cut in a pure Roman.

And Nicolas Jenson was not far behind him. This
former master of the mint at Tours, who, we remember,
had been sent to Mainz in 1458 by the French king to learn
Gutenberg's secret, had returned to France in 1461. Find-
ing that the son of Charles VII, who had succeeded to the
French throne, was not interested in the new art, he emi-
grated to Italy where he met with much more enthusiasm.

Some time before 1470 he started printing in Venice.
He so perfected the roman small letters that his type forms
became models not only for printers in his own day but for
all since who have cared for the beautiful letter forms.

abcdefgh

Jenson's type was beautiful, and the letters fitted
harmoniously together on the page because he did not try
to imitate handwriting, as did so many of the early printers
and type-cutters, but accepted honestly the medium in
which he worked. He took as inspiration a fine manuscript
hand, but only as inspiration, and then worked as an independent craftsman in metal. He did not try to follow the
pen style slavishly.

This French maker of coins and types brought much glory to Venice, and his fame spread beyond the city of canals. Another Venetian who followed him and used his fonts of type, however, won even greater fame both as printer and type designer. Aldus Manutius was his name.

Aldus, as he is commonly called now, put more care into the designing and setting and arranging of his type and the actual printing than had most of his predecessors. He produced some of the finest books of all times. Others had printed large books; he made small and cheap ones, well printed and easy to read. A special type that he designed for these little books, based on a slanted "familiar," or local, handwriting was the first *italic* type. He had earlier produced a slanted Greek alphabet for his small volumes of the classics. These hit the popular taste and increased the fame of the Aldine press. The pocket books, or "Aldine

Abcdefgh

Κολοφῶνι μα

classics," one of the most famous of which was the little volume of the Latin poet Virgil, set a fashion in small, inexpensive, but attractively printed books which has continued, or perhaps one should say has been revived from time to time, to our own day. It is one of the many things for which we can gratefully remember Aldus.

Aldus designed a "trade mark" to be printed in all his books so that everyone would know they were his work. Many publishers and printers followed this practice. If only Gutenberg had done the same, what a lot of puzzling and guesswork would have been spared! The first such mark was that of Fust and Schoeffer—the two shields which they used in their Psalter of 1457. At first books had carried no date, no title page, nothing that would indicate when or by whom the work was done. Then, following the custom of many of the scribes, printers began putting at the end of the work the name of the producer, the date and place of production, and sometimes other information about the type and method of work. This came later to be called a "colophon," from the Greek word meaning a "finishing stroke." It was not until after 1520 that the custom of putting such information on a title page became common.

This famous printer's mark, the dolphin and anchor of the Aldine Press, first used in 1502, symbolized speed and firmness. The various monogram and symbolic picture designs as well as the simpler racing hounds and penguins and kangaroos and whales that are the trade marks of some modern publishers and printing houses are direct descendants of such early printers' marks.

Since the first use of Aldus' italic type, which became immensely popular when he used it in the volume of Virgil in 1501, there has been no new *style* of letter that has been accepted for standard use up to our own day. In our books henceforth there will be just these: italic capitals and small letters and roman capitals and small letters, though there are hundreds of variations of all of them. Of course there is also the Black Letter, and in very recent times such modern forms as sans-serif and square-serif and even-weight alphabets have been produced. These latter, until time approves or disapproves, must be considered in the same light as any other contemporary fad—not as a basic letter design.

Capitals and small letters are known by printers as upper-case and lower-case letters from the practice of keeping the capitals in the upper part of the storage tray (or case) and the small letters in the lower part.

While the roman letters were developing to such perfection in the printed books of Italy, the first printers in France, probably because they came from Germany as their names indicate—Friburger, Gering, and Krantz—started compromise styles known as the "lettres batarde." Though these alphabets resembled the Gothic in the sharpness of their angles, the French types were not so heavy and dark as the Black Letter types of other countries. There was a leaning toward the lighter and more delicate Roman letters. The *batarde* forms, so characteristically French—sharp but light and spirited—continued to dominate French printing for many years.

The other French styles most often met in early printing are known as *de forme*.

Almost everywhere else in Europe, however, for more than a hundred years after Gutenberg worked in Mainz,

and much longer than that in some countries, the Gothic
style prevailed. Variations of the style were many; here
are only two (a "fracture" and a "Schwabacher") to indicate how widely Black Letter forms could differ.

Hamburg

Hamburg

Printing first came to the Low Countries in 1473, if,
of course, we neglect the claims of Coster. The Dutch
printers were mainly responsible for many of the fine
Gothic letters we have today. In their hands the letters
became less monotonously parallel and squeezed, fuller and
more finished, and varied and graceful in their lines. One

ABC FPL

dacht te vgadere

of the finest workmen in Holland in the fifteenth century was a man named Enschede. And there were many famous names among the printers of the Netherlands in the next century. One of the best known is Christophe Plantin, who worked in Antwerp.

Printing was introduced in Spain in 1474. We saw that even in the days of the scribes, when the national hands were being developed, the Spanish were fond of ornate

bastarda ALg Ciardi Ha

Redondilla Llana Giouan

redondo de libros non

letters with many fancy turns and fine flourishes. After the first presses started there, the Spanish developed type styles that resembled their writing styles. Although they began with the Gothic, it soon became very Spanish. Spanish books have a character all their own, a kind of bold sweep that reminds one of the plumes of the grandees in the days of Columbus. Even when they used roman letters, they "Spanished" them in much the same way.

The father of English printing was William Caxton. We know more about his history, fortunately, than we do of Gutenberg and many other early printers. Born in Eng-

land about 1422, he became a mercer, or cloth merchant, and for many years traveled abroad, principally in Germany and the Low Countries. His chief residence was in the ancient Flemish city of Bruges in what is now Belgium, which at that time was a great center of weaving and cloth making. For some time he was governor of the Merchant Adventurers in the Low Countries, a group otherwise known as "The English Nation," composed of English merchants living abroad. He also served as a kind of English ambassador in Bruges to the court of the dukes of Burgundy who then controlled the country. There he had access to a rich library, in which were undoubtedly many examples of the new art of printing.

Caxton was so interested in this new way of making books and saw such great possibilities in it that he went to Cologne in 1471-1472 to learn the trade. Then in 1474 he set up a press in Bruges and with the aid of a famous French scribe, Colard Mansion, designed and cut the first

"English type." It wasn't, strictly speaking, English; it was really a kind of Dutch Gothic that Caxton introduced into England. In 1475 or 1476 Caxton produced in Bruges the first book ever to be printed in English. It was his own translation from the French of a collection of popular French romances based on the history of Troy.

Caxton was well past fifty years of age when he entered upon the profession that was to bring him great fame and the world much pleasure and information. At the end of the book in a kind of epilogue or colophon he says, "my penne is worn, myn hand wery and not stedfast, myn eyn dimed with over moche looking on whit paper, and my corage not so prone and redy to laboure as hit hath been, and . . . age crepeth on me dayly and feebleth all the bodye." But he adds, as if proud of the new art he has learned and

¶ Here begynneth the boke Intituled Eracles, and also of Godfrey of Bolyne, the whiche speketh of the Conquest of the holy londe of Jherusalem, contenyng diuerse warres and noble faytes of Armes made in the same Royame, and in the contrees adiacent. And also many meruayllous werkes happed and fallen as wel on this syde as in tho partyes this tyme durynge. And how the valyant duc Godefrey of Bolyne conquerd with the swerd the sayd Royamme, And was kynge there,

¶ The ffirst chapitre treateth how Eracles conquerd Perse and slewe Cosdroe, and brought in to Jherusalem the very crosse, capitulo primo,

The Auncyent hystoryes saye that Eracles was a good crysten man and gouernour of thempyre of Rome, But in his tyme Machomet had ben whiche was messager of the deuil And made the peple to vnderstonde, that he was a prophete sent from our lorde, In the tyme of Eracles was the fals lawe of machomet sowen and sprad abrode in many partyes of thoryent, and

in this fair boke/that ye wyl remēbre how the poure soules be
leyed in the fyre of purgatorie. And therwyth he departed: whā
the clerke was leyed down in his fair bode he myght neither sle
pe ne reste whan he remembred the wordes that the prechour
had said to hym On the morn whan he was rysen he gat all
that he had for the loue of god & entred in to relygyon:& after
was an holy man/ Now seest thou how it is good to here the
word of god/It is slouthe whan thou goost not gladly ne w
ith a good wyll to chirche. For it is the first thyng that thou
oughtest to doo whan thou art rysen out of thy bedde for to re
comande the to god/& in good trouthe thou & all thy werkes &
besynesses shall fare the better yf thou so doo . Example Elea
zar whyche was patriarke of alexandrie recounteth of two cor
dewaners whiche were gossybs & liueden by their crafte. That
one was right a good werke man and had not grete meincy
in his hous..and was alle way poure.& alle way he cessed not
to werke/That other was no good werkman & had a grete
houshold and grete meincy.but he doubted moche our lord god.

For it is the first

conscious of the great benefits that would come from making books available to everyone, "it is not wreton with
penne and ynke as other bokes ben," but "begonne on oon
day and also finished in oon day."

In 1477 Caxton returned to England with a new font
of improved type and set up his press in Westminster, then
a suburb of London. The following year he produced the
first book printed on English soil, *The Dictes and Sayings
of the Philosophres*. From that time on he was busy, in

spite of his "dimed eyn," writing, revising, translating, making types, and printing until his death about 1491. Among the famous books that he printed were Chaucer's *Canterbury Tales* and *Malory's Morte d'Arthur*, for which he wrote a famous preface supporting the view that there really was a King Arthur.

Caxton used about eight fonts of type, one of them a copy of the type used by Fust and Schoeffer. His letters were ornate but readable and beautiful on the page. It is English Gothic or "Old English" at its finest.

The influence of Caxton was so great that black letters continued for several centuries to be the preferred type for charters, acts of Parliament, legal documents, and church literature. Even today much church printing, and many documents such as diplomas are done in this style.

The Caxton tradition was carried on by Wynkyn de Worde, who had come to England as his helper. De Worde used Caxton's types in over seven hundred books.

It is not strange that the black letter had so strong a hold on European printing. There are several reasons for it, the most powerful of which, as we might expect, being custom. The ordinary book buyer and reader in northern countries was used to the bold black text of the Gothic. Even Jenson, who had designed a fine Roman letter, was forced to print in Gothic to make his books more salable to northern readers. Then, too, the lighter roman types were open and round and it was thought at first that they had to be printed in large sizes to be readable. Fewer words were set to the page and the cost of large books was hence increased.

In the sixteenth century roman type finally did triumph almost everywhere in Europe except Germany—even in conservative England. One who helped much in the change from black letter to roman was the English printer John Day, who in 1572, while Queen Elizabeth was on the throne, cut a fine large roman type and used it in several books. His printer's mark on the title page was a pun on his own name—a sleeping man awakened by the rising sun, with the words: "Arise for it is Day."

Juan Pablos set up the first printing press in the Western Hemisphere, in Mexico City in 1539, only twenty years after Cortez landed. Although he himself was an Italian, he used Spanish Gothic types, for he was an agent of a printer in Seville, Spain. When printing came to the American colonies, however, just a hundred years later, the types were brought from England where by that time

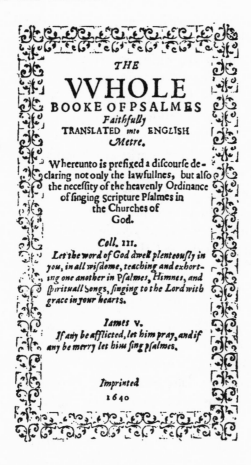

roman letters were in common use. So the first book printed in what is now the United States, the *Bay Psalm Book* of 1640, the work of Stephen Daye, was done in roman letters, which ever since have governed our styles and tastes. In the three hundred years of American printing we have borrowed all the features of English type designs, good and bad. Only fairly recently—in fact, in the present century in which we live—have we begun to create types of our own that are individual and distinctive.

In the later sixteenth century in England, and indeed throughout Europe, the quality of type styles began to get very poor. One of the chief reasons was that as the scribes became less important to the men who worked in type, they were employed less and were not able to keep up the high quality of contemporary calligraphy. Whereas before they had created the forms upon which the type designers and printers based their work, and then for some time had been considered indispensable for decorating and initialing and finishing the printed books, now they became little more than second-rate printers' helpers. When printers made new types, they no longer went to the scribes for their inspiration. Type cutters denied the tradition of fine writing. Instead of working from some good manuscript, they took for their models types already designed, very often not the best ones. Then, too, the third generation of printers was very often composed of ordinary men, without the skilled hand or the artistic eye of Nicolas Jenson, or the learning or taste of Aldus. Printing had become so common that it was a trade and no longer an art as it most often had been in the hands of the great printers of the fifteenth and early sixteenth centuries.

An interest in, and an appreciation for, the decorative value of letters never was lost, however, even in the worst times. As evidence, look at this limited assortment of English, Scottish, Spanish, and Dutch designs. They range from

CIVI · PROBO · ER · QVÆSTORI

29 · MAII · A · D · 1606 · ÆT · SVÆ ·

Scottish inscription

English bell inscription

English warming pan

Spanish ironwork

Dutch Canon

English furniture

inscriptions on bells and canon right down to furniture and warming pans!

The earliest types were beautiful mainly because they had been based on good *written* letters. But what could be expected of copies several times removed from the original forms? When things got so bad that they could hardly be worse, a few particular readers began to demand something better in their printed books. As an answer, the *writing master* came forward to try to improve the quality of hands in general use and, through this educational process, the type faces. A whole set of letter styles grew up during the sixteenth century. Little "writing books" were prepared and published to show the new styles that thus developed.

But while the letters of the printers had become dull and unimaginative and ugly, unpleasing to the eye and difficult to read, the writing masters frequently went to the other extreme and developed alphabets that for flowery frills were a wonder to behold!

Here are a few of the letters recommended by these masters of the sixteenth century.

First was an "Imperialle," perhaps the most elaborate of all, not very readable and used mostly for the decorative parts of a book or manuscript.

The second was a "fiammanga," meaning "Flemish" (below and at the top of page 236). It also was used for decorative writing and inscriptions. The example on the next page is taken from a drug pot.

The third style, called "moderne," was a more simple, strong, and rather handsome alphabet used mostly for engraving on wood.

The fourth included a whole group of "chancery scripts," styles developed for use in church writing. Three of them are shown here (below and at the top of the next page).

The fifth group included all the manuscript hands. Some of these were simple, readable, and usable enough, often approaching the beauty and grace of some of the best work of the scribes in the days before printing. One of the

gratíam / Delegar

concede

magnam & predica

genitore meo et gen

textura

very best of these letters for book work came from a place
where we would least expect such simplicity—Spain. This
"antigua" letter was about as fine as anything that was done
anywhere in Europe.

Letra Antigua Ron

A little more decorative, but still simpler than most
Spanish alphabets were the letters of the best Spanish scribes
of the sixteenth century. Really fine book hands were shown
in Juan de Yciar's writing book in 1570.

Unfortunately, however, the best of the writing masters
had very little permanent influence on printing, particularly in England. There it got worse and worse and reached
its lowest ebb in the seventeenth century. The Puritan
middle classes cared very little for beauty in things of every
day life; their main concern was for utility. When they did
go in for decoration in letters, they showed very bad taste.

In some places, especially Germany, letters were taking
the forms they were to keep for more than two hundred
years. Seventeenth-century German type styles were almost
identical with those in use today.

In the eighteenth century two great type designers drew English printing, at least temporarily, out of the depths of dullness and ugliness into which it had fallen.

The first of these was the Englishman, William Caslon, whose business was casting, or "founding," type. Like Nicolas Jenson, Caslon had the skilled eye and hand of an engraver, for he had started as a maker of gun locks, which were then all engraved by hand. About 1724 he designed a type that came to be known as "Caslon Old Face," based largely on the fine letter forms of Jenson but a little less black and heavy, showing the free work of a fine artist. He not only revived the excellent design and spirit of the golden age of Italian printing in the fifteenth century but put new life and variety into the printing of his own day. The individual letters look very commonplace now, partly because we are so familiar with them. No type of any time, however, has ever made a more attractive and readable page than the original type of Caslon—not, it must be added, the often badly cut and distorted imitations of the nineteenth and twentieth centuries.

You have an example of a modern redrawing of Caslon's fine old type, his honest, handsome letters, before you now as you read this book, which is set in the alphabet he designed more than two hundred years ago.

The other style of roman type designed in the eighteenth century, which had an even greater influence than the "old-style" of Caslon for a while, was what came to be known in the late eighteenth and early nineteenth centuries as *modern*. Its most successful designer, perhaps, was Giambattista Bodoni, an Italian printer working at Parma. Bodoni's *modern* letters have no gradual shading of thick lines or curves into thin as have the *oldstyle;* the thicks are very thick and black and the thins are almost hairlines. The serifs, instead of rounding gradually into the stem,

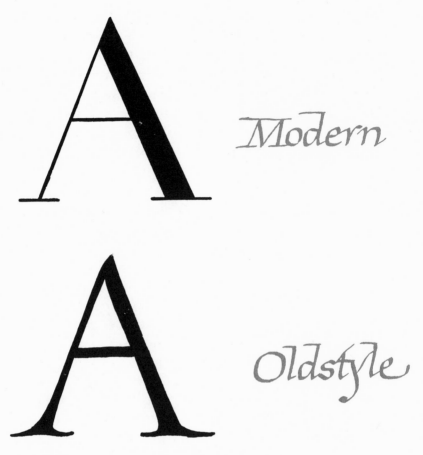

Modern

Oldstyle

are squared off at the ends of the main strokes. Bodoni's letters make an elegant, sparkling page but not so readable as one of Caslon's. The contrasts between thick and thin are too extreme, and the primness of exact balance, thought to be "classical" in the eighteenth century, does not so much appeal to our eyes.

Nineteenth-century printing was very dreary for the most part. It ran from the small type and crowded pages of the "penny magazines" and other cheap work in the earlier machine age to the gingerbread letters of late Victorian times. The printer Baskerville carried on the modern tradi-

The Bauer Type Foundry's Bodoni

tion started by Bodoni. However, in its use by others less skillful than its designer, the Baskerville family became very monotonous.

Some relief from bad printing came after 1844 when the younger Charles Whittingham of the Chiswick Press revived several Caslon fonts and cut a new oldstyle. William Morris, who did much for the revival of fine printing and excellent letter design toward the end of the century, learned his trade at the Chiswick Press.

The most important developments in the nineteenth century affecting the production of books were certain mechanical inventions. With the demand for quantity production the individual workman was rapidly losing control of the tools. That perhaps accounts for much of the bad printing of the time. It is only in the present century that we have sufficiently brought the tools again under the control of intelligent, artistic, competent craftsmen that we are producing really fine letters in beautiful books.

The Industrial Revolution, which came to England shortly before 1800 and which was to have so great an effect on life in the next century, first made itself felt in the printing business in 1814. In that year Frederick Koenig built for the *London Times* two printing presses which ran by steam power. Instead of a top speed of 250 sheets an hour, which was the very best that hand presses could maintain, the new steam presses printed 1100 sheets an hour. This seems nothing now in comparison with our big newspaper presses which run off 60,000 sheets an hour, but it was the beginning of an era of speed. The introduction of the machine was immensely important to the whole bookmaking profession and finally, of course, to the character of the letters themselves.

The essential forms of the letters were not changed by the use of machines, but new ways of making type and

setting and printing it did affect their *design* and their artistic appearance on the page. It is impossible even to mention here all the improvements and changes that were made to speed up the printing process. It was only later, and sometimes as an afterthought, that attention was turned to the improvement of the letters themselves and their appearance on the page.

The old ink rollers were replaced by ones made of molasses and glue, which inked faster and more evenly. Paper was fed into the presses automatically from great rolls and was cut into sheets only after the printing was completed. Just before the twentieth century a way was discovered to make curved printing plates so that they fit around a roller. The paper then ran from one roller to another, which brought it in contact with the inked cylinder that did the printing, increasing the speed a hundred fold.

The result of these, and many other, inventions was that

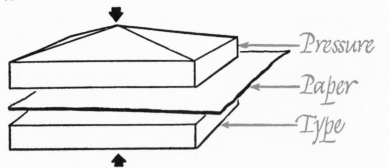

Pressure

Paper

Type

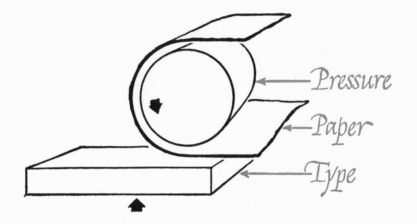

Pressure

Paper

Type

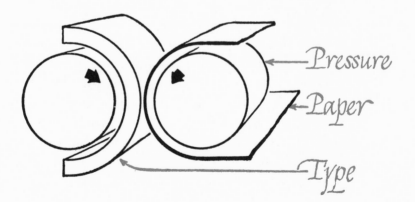

Pressure

Paper

Type

printing was now done so fast that the typesetters could no longer keep up with the presses. One of these speedy presses required an army of men setting type to supply it. There was a limit to the speed with which even the most skilled compositor could set a page of type. In 1882 a machine was invented which cast type automatically. This developed into what we call the "monotype" machine, which not only casts but also sets the individual type pieces in the line.

The first typesetting machine which set and cast an entire line was patented in 1885 by Ottmar Mergenthaler, a

German-American watchmaker, who had worked on the device for many years before it was ready for practical use. It is a very intricate mechanical device. Watching an operator work this "linotype," as it is called, gives one a

Early Linotype

Later Linotype

feeling that it is almost human in its movements. The
operator presses the keys on a keyboard, similar to that of
a typewriter, and the machine does all the rest. It picks

out each matrix from a magazine containing many matrices of each character; it places the matrix in the line; and, when the line is completed, it spaces the words to bring each line to a uniform width. Then, after the lead has poured into the mold containing the matrices, making a solid line of type, a long arm picks up the matrices and returns them, without ever an error, to their proper places in the magazine. The Linotype machine works five times as fast as the speediest hand type setter.

As a result of all these mechanical inventions, the modern production of printed words has increased to the point where it is impossible to realize the significance of the figures we must deal with. In one day in America there are more than forty million newspapers printed. The total number of words printed in them, daily, is greater than all the words in all recorded literature before the invention of printing. And this doesn't include the millions of books printed every year or the countless magazines!

Now let us see what the increased speed and the mechanical production of books has done to our alphabet. In the nineteenth century the first crude use of machines, not so perfect and precise in their operation as they later became, naturally made for poorer type and press work than had formerly come from the best of the hand printers. The fine lines and subtle curves of the designer were often lost in the mechanical operations of the new punch cutters. This, coupled with the unintelligent copying of copies of earlier types caused a reaction toward hand work among those who, like William Morris, cared about the beauty of letters and fine printing.

Morris believed that nothing good could come from the machine. It seemed to him to give no play to the artistic impulse, and all its creations were alike in dullness. He set about making new type designs and doing his own hand

such as choose to seek it: it is neither
prison, nor palace, but a decent home.
ALL WHICH I NEI-
THER praise. nor
blame, but say that
so it is: some people
praise this homeli-
ness overmuch, as
if the land were the
very axle-tree of the
world; so do not I, nor any unblind-
ed by pride in themselves and all that
belongs to them: others there are who
scorn it and the tameness of it: not
I any the more: though it would indeed be hard if there were nothing
else in the world, no wonders, no ter-
rors, no unspeakable beauties. Yet
when we think what a small part of
the world's history, past, present, &
to come, is this land we live in, and
how much smaller still in the history
of the arts, & yet how our forefathers
clung to it, and with what care and

"Troy" type

THE ARGUMENT.

UCIUS Tarquinius (for his exces-sive pride surnamed Superbus) af-ter hee had caused his owne father in law Servius Tullius to be cruelly murd'red, and contrarie to the Ro-maine lawes and customes, not re-quiring or staying for the people's suffrages, had possessed himselfe of the kingdome: went accom-panyed with his sonnes and other noble men of Rome, to besiege Ardea, during which siege, the principall men of the Army meeting one evening at the tent of Sextus Tarquinius the king's sonne, in their discourses after supper every one commen-ded the vertues of his owne wife: among whom Colatinus extolled the incomparable chastity of his wife Lucretia. In that pleasant humor they all posted to Rome, & intending by theyr secret and sodaine arrivall to make triall of that which every one had before avouched, onely Colatinus finds his wife (though it were late in the night) spinning amongest her maides, the other ladies were all found dauncing and revelling, or in severall dis-ports: whereupon the noble men yeelded Cola-tinus the victory, and his wife the fame. At that time Sextus Tarquinius being enflamed with Lu-crece beauty, yet smoothering his passions for the present, departed with the rest backe to the campe:

"Golden" type

printing at his now famous Kelmscott Press. Turning for his models back to the Middle Ages, when hand work was at its finest, he designed a Gothic type from which he printed an edition of Chaucer's *Canterbury Tales*, decorating the margins and making elaborate initial letters in the manner of the medieval scribes. It was one of the finest books printed in the nineteenth century, but his Gothic type was not very practical for everyday use.

More useful was his "golden type," inspired by the fine roman letters of Nicolas Jenson. It had, also, more influence upon the renewed interest in handsome simple letter designs that was to break out in England in the 1890's. This interest in fine printing spread to America soon after and, before our day, caused such a change for the better in printed letter forms that some have called it a "second Renaissance."

Of course there is now and there probably always will be much bad printing, just as there is bad taste in a great many other things of everyday use. The gratifying thing is that this new birth of excellent taste and the preference for fine, simple, and beautiful types has spread beyond such private pressmen as William Morris and his followers. It has had its effect on publishers of books and magazines and newspapers and even on advertisers. Not only expensive books but even the cheapest are today more handsome and more readable than books in general have ever been before.

How did such a transformation come about? In the first place, publishers began employing better men, real artists, to do their lettering and book design; and type founders selected careful workmen to cut and cast their type. True artists, too, entered the field of type designing, men of skill and knowledge of the history of letters who went to the best models of the past, to the Trajan capitals, to the finest hands of the medieval scribes, to the most perfect letters in the golden age of printing. The reading public, faced with a choice of good or poor printing has found *its* good taste again, too, and is beginning to demand good work.

We have looked, as we have gone along, at many different alphabets. We have seen how they grew and changed since those first Roman capital letters. Since the invention of printing we have looked mostly at type designs. Some of them were good and are still in use today. Some of them were bad. The poor ones influenced the work of their time a little and then they were forgotten.

Out of all these many, many alphabet designs—the originals and the copies, the good and the bad, the new and the old—we find only a very few which are important enough to be called "styles."

On the next few pages are some modern types and a page of calligraphic letters. These are by no means *all* the best types that modern type foundries are producing—each year there are more—nor are these the only hands that one should be able to write well. If we can decide, however, why these types are sound, and if we can learn to write like these calligraphic lines, we shall have grown in taste and knowledge to a point where we can decide for ourselves what is good and what is bad—and why.

CANTO QUINTO
ARGOMENTO

Solve il dubbio d'intorno a'voti, mosso nel canto di sopra: poi sale al
secondo cielo che è quel di Mercurio, dove trova infinite anime, una delle
quali se gli offerisce a soddisfare ad ogni sua dimanda

S'io ti fiammeggio nel caldo d'amore   1
Di là dal modo che'n terra si vede,
Sicchè degli occhi tuoi vinco'l valore,
Non ti maravigliar; che ciò procede   4

Type Tables

Here at last, the masterpiece of the designer, E. R. Weiss

WEISS ROMAN

From top to bottom: Bodoni, Legend, Weiss

THIS TRAJAN   This face is tried

The

Merchant of
Venice

abcdefghijklmnopqrstuvwxyz
ABCDEFGHIJKLMNOPQRSTUVWXYZ

EARNEST MARINER
mechanics complimented

ABCDEFGHIJKLM
NOPRSTUVWXYZ
abcdefghijklmnopqrst
uvwxyz &1234567890$

Trajan, Medieval, Caslon, Spartan,
Bulmer, Garamond

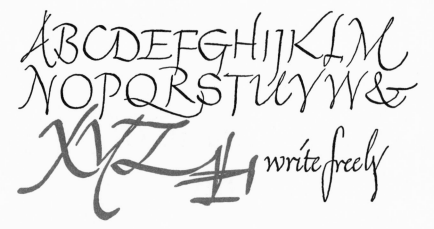

ABCDEFGHIJKLM
NOPQRSTUVYW&
XYZ write freely

WRITE UNCIALS

FLAT PEN CAPS

Always write carefully, whether you write large or sma

There are only 26
...use them wisely

Chapter 10

THE ALPHABET TODAY

During the two decades following this book's original publication, a host of artists conducted many new and challenging experiments with our letter forms.

The works of some of these men have enhanced the usefulness of the alphabet and have helped to keep it in the mainstream of modern thinking. One should mention here types such as Hermann Zapf's Palatino and Melior, Warren Chappell's Trajanus, Jan Tschichold's Sabon Antiqua, and the magnificent redrawing of sixteenth-century Garamond by the D. Stampel Foundry in Germany—all adapted from traditional roman forms. There were also new experiments with sans serif types such as Folio, Univers, and Helvetica, which followed the pioneer Paul Renner's Futura, as well as Photo-Lettering alphabets like Squire, drawn by Hollis Holland several years ago, to list only a few.

ABCDEFGHIJKLMN OPQRSTUVWXYZ abcdefghijklmno

Palatino

Historiographer HORSE

Corned beef FEAR

Forum of Youth

Melior

ABCDEFGHIJKLMNOP
QRSTUVWXYZ
abcdefghijklmnopqrstuv

Trajanus

ABCDEFGHIJKLMNOPQ
RSTUVWXYZÄÖÜ
abcdefghijklmnopqrstuvwxyz
ßchckfffiflft&äöü
1234567890 1234567890
.,:;-!?.'()[]*†‹›»«„",”/£$

Sabon Antiqua

Filmaufnahme KORFU

Boekenkast LENZ

Schweden ROM

Garamond

Declaration, without distinct

ion of any kind such as

race, colour, relig

ion, language

Folio

abcdefghjklmnopqrtu

ABCDEFGHJKLMNQ

abcdeghijklmnopqrstuvwxyz

ABCDEFGHJKLMNOPQRSY

abcdefghijklmnopqrstuvwxyzabcd

Univers

ABCDEFGHIJKL
abcdefghijklmno

ABCDEFGHIJKLMO
abcdefghijkmnopqrs

Helvetica

SQUIRE Squire
Photo-Lettering
PHOTO-LETTERING

Squire

On the other hand, some truly far-out designs and some farfetched "psychedelic," *art nouveau* typographic fads came into being but will soon, one assumes as with most temporary fads, be going on their way.

PSYCHEDELITYPE ALPHABET
PSYCHEDELITYPE ALPHABET

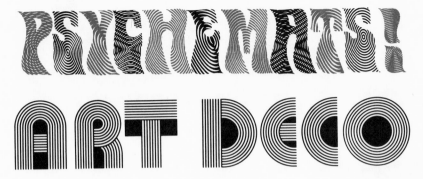

Of course, the designers of these unusual characters are not the first in the long history of the alphabet to devote themselves wholeheartedly to a new or different notion.

For instance, at about the time of the First World War, a school in Germany known as the Bauhaus and headed by the architect Walter Gropius was established with the express purpose of revolutionizing all the arts—including the art of the letter—by teaching that the pure arts must be combined with the crafts. "Functional craftsmanship," it was called, and it took into account the ways in which artists and craftsmen can cooperate with machines and mass-production methods.

The influence of the school was so great that it affected every form of art and design from architecture and furniture to weaving and typography.

Naturally, so revolutionary an approach found opposition among academicians and politicians. The school was forced to move from its home town, Weimar, to Dessau and finally to Berlin. The teachings, however, gained wide support in the United States and some of the teachers, under artist-craftsman Moholy-Nagy, came here and founded in 1939 a Bauhaus school known as the Chicago Institute of Design.

Some Bauhaus influences still linger in the arts today—the Futura type mentioned earlier is a fine example.

ABCDEFGHIJKLMNOPQRSTUVWXYZ

abcdefghijklmnopqrstuvwxyz

1234567890

Futura

Another great revolutionary—whom you have met before—was William Morris, born in 1834, who felt that the arts and crafts of his time were being threatened by mechanization. He was reacting, as we have seen, against the first crude use of machines in the nineteenth century.

Morris threw in his fortunes with poet Dante Gabriel Rossetti's Pre-Raphaelite reform movement. The reformers sought to deny the machine and all its works by reviving the arts and crafts of the Middle Ages.

William Morris devoted himself to the promotion of hand-made everything—carvings, stained glass, carpets, wallpaper, chintzes, even furniture. Did you ever see a Morris chair? It is a clumsy reclining monstrosity of wood and leather—but very comfortable.

Finally, in about 1890, Morris set up the Kelmscott Press to adapt his philosophy to book production. His arbitrary, inefficient, and downright reactionary ideas became as popular in his day as similar reversions to *art nouveau* have today. They greatly influenced letter designers of the late nineteenth and early twentieth centuries but eventually lost out to the irresistible forces of mechanization, which tend to require simpler, cleaner forms.

From the modern designer's standpoint, the Pre-Raphaelites did no permanent harm—they may even have opened some eyes to the values of human involvement and to the danger of their being eliminated by the impersonal machine. Neither, we can be sure, will today's faddish designers do any long-range damage. Some muscle-bound old traditionalists find it hard to tolerate the new revolution. However, it may loosen them up—make them more sensitive to the creative potential of their own work.

At any rate, it is safe to say that no permanent changes have yet come to our alphabet since it was frozen so many years ago into its present form. In recent years letters have at times been thickened and thinned and twisted and contorted and punished and embarrassed by letterers who cater to current fashion, but there are, fortunately—and will surely be in the years ahead—enough informed and concerned artists to keep the beauty and legibility of well-drawn, tradition-founded letters before the reader.

ART NOUUEAU EXTRAVAGANZA

A BARREL OF LAUGHS

∎∎ FIRST NATIONAL BANK ∎∎

MORE DESIGNATED

WASHINGTON ARCH opening

SPY CONFESSES

contemporary !

Of course, the shapes of letters are partly determined by methods of printing as well as by fads and fashions. Just as the shapes of letters in the past were influenced by the tools used in their production, so today we find that the forms of our letters are responding to changes in printing techniques.

In general, during the years since the introduction of movable type in Europe back in the fifteenth century, only three basic methods for printing have been devised.

First, of course, is relief, or *letterpress*, printing. This is the original method for repeating designs on paper— first used by the Chinese in the first century of the Christian era and adopted by the Western world when printing was introduced there. In this process, as we have seen, the printing surface is raised above the remainder of the plate, is inked, and an impression is made on paper.

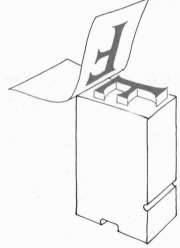

Letterpress

Second is *intaglio*, employed in etching, gravure, and other methods where the printing surface is sunk *below* the remainder of the plate. The indentations are filled with ink, the rest of the plate is wiped clean; and the paper, when pressed upon the plate, absorbs the ink from the depressions.

Intaglio

Third is *planographic*, in which the printing surface and the rest of the plate are practically the same height. Ink adheres only where the plate has been treated to accept it and is repelled elsewhere. This method, commonly known as lithography, has become generally accepted for much contemporary printing in its offset form.

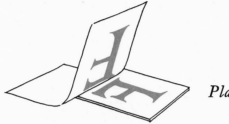

Planographic

Perhaps the most important development in the printing industry in recent years is the replacement to a large degree of the letterpress process, formerly the most widely employed method, by lithography.

Four kinds of planographic printing are in use today.

The original was *stone lithography*, an accidental discovery of Aloys Senefelder, who was born in Prague in 1771, and whose father was associated with the Theatre Royale.

One of Aloys' duties as a young man was to reproduce theater bills and programs for his father. He used copper plates (intaglio), but they were expensive and required a very long time to engrave. The plates could be reused, but first they had to be resurfaced, and this also took a long time.

For practicing mirror-image writing—which was, of course, called for if the letters on the printed sheet were to appear right side up and read normally left-to-right—

Theatre Royale

he often used a smooth piece of Kelheim stone, a special form of Bavarian sandstone, and wrote with ink made of wax, soap, and lampblack. The stones, used for polishing his copper plates, were easily cleaned, and they made good, inexpensive practice pads.

One day his mother asked him to figure out a bill for the washerwoman who was waiting with the linen. Having at hand no pen and paper, he worked out the account on a handy Kelheim stone.

Sometime later when he went to clean the stone, the idea came to him to try "biting" it with aquafortis as he did his copper plates. After about five minutes, he noticed that the writing stood a tiny bit above the surrounding area (it was actually only about two-hundredths of an inch). He proceeded to flush the stone with water to prevent further action of the acid and applied with a roller the same kind of ink he had used for the laundry bill. He found that the ink adhered only to the writing—not to the damp open areas of the stone—and that by pressing a sheet of paper upon it he could get a very satisfactory print.

For years Senefelder continued his experiments, perfecting his stone-writing and printing techniques. Lithography, incidentally, *is* stone-writing: "lithos" for *stone;* "graphos" for *writing.* He was never able to get a patent, but he guided the process to such a high degree of excellence that it was widely adopted for both artistic and commercial uses.

A commercial lithographic press of the 1850's

As a belated reward for his contribution, the king of Bavaria eventually settled a handsome pension on Aloys Senefelder and made his old age a comfortable one.

Stone lithography is now used only for handdrawn and manually printed illustrations and fine art prints.

The next commercial application of planographic printing to develop was *direct lithography*, in which plates of various metals, treated with light-sensitive albumin coatings, were substituted for the heavy stones.

The image to be printed is photographed onto the plate, which has been so sensitized and treated that it accepts ink only where the image has been exposed.

In direct lithography, printing is done by impressing the paper directly onto the plate. The rather frail image in the coating is easily damaged during the printing process, however, so the number of prints obtainable is relatively few.

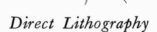

Direct Lithography

The third form of planographic printing is *offset lithography*—so called because the image on the plate does not come into direct contact with the paper but, after inking, is transferred (offset) to a rubber or composition blanket which in turn becomes the actual printing surface.

This is the method now so generally used for commercial printing—the one that has nearly replaced the traditional letterpress. It is extremely versatile and can be used for practically any kind of printed item from gallery reproductions, advertising promotions, posters, packages and greeting cards, to magazines, newspapers, and books.

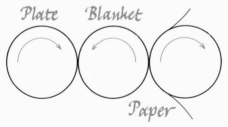

Offset Lithography

With offset lithography, extremely long print runs are possible. Whereas direct lithography usually has a limit of a few thousand impressions per plate, offset print runs of several hundred thousand are possible, using presensitized wipe-on or deep-etched plates. With bimetal plates (in which the areas to be printed and those which are not to be printed are different metals) runs of several million impressions are possible.

The fourth form of planographic printing is *porous printing*, known also as silk screen. The screen is a porous cloth (originally silk, hence the name) stretched tightly across a frame. Ink is flowed onto this screen and forced through the openings with a kind of squeegee. Openings in the cloth are blocked out by applying cutout film where no ink is to seep through onto the paper below. Blocking-out can also be done by painting on a compound called touche which fills the openings of the screen and thus prevents ink from reaching the paper.

With special inks, this process can be used to print on almost any surface—paper, plastics, metal foil, sheet metal, fiber glass, fiberboard, wood, or even (if you're interested) drums of Swiss cheese.

Silk Screen

The layer of ink forced through the screen is usually heavier than that used in other kinds of printing. This is especially true when the new fluorescent inks are called for. When transparent inks are used—overprinting each other for various color effects—thinner inks are forced through the screen and very sophisticated blocking out is employed.

The fine-art variety of porous printing is called *serigraphy*, now used by many artists for print-making—and with exciting results. The name is an American contribution. Serigraphy is becoming ever more popular in this country and is rapidly spreading to Europe and Asia.

*   *   *

Now, to get back to that printing process that has grown so remarkably in recent years: offset lithography. Techniques, equipment, and the know-how of workers have improved so vastly in the past twenty-odd years that it is no longer a poor relation of letterpress—a printing process to be used only for economy work of low quality. As a matter of fact, this new edition of *The 26 Letters* has been converted to offset from pages of the early letterpress edition. Some of the most distinguished full-color printing ever produced is now being done on huge, speedy, multi-color, automated offset presses. Beautiful work, in many ways superior to the finest letterpress, is being "litho'd" throughout the world.

Many of the old "hot metal" designers (your author is one) deplore the passing of the exciting character of a printed page that can come only from well-designed metal type, properly set and carefully impressed into dampened, hand-made paper. We also regret this break in the continuity of letterpress work from the earliest days of the craft. However, the old should give way to the young;

the traditional should adapt to the present. Tastes change, economic conditions change, printing requirements change; it is the duty of those who are involved in the graphic arts to make use of, and to guide into proper channels—not refuse to accept—the new experiments.

To make full use of planographic printing, the physical setting of metal type has been gradually giving way to new methods of type composition which use no metal at all. For printing without impressions, the industry is developing typesetting without type!

As we have seen, in offset printing the plate is prepared photographically; type itself never touches the paper—its only purpose is to supply images to be photographed. When metal type is to be the source of this image, it is set in the usual way, a careful reproduction proof is made, and this proof is used for photography. Thus, the quality of the final offset plate is entirely dependent upon the quality of the reproduction proof.

Now, wholly photographic composing methods, called photocomposition, have been developed, eliminating the need for reproduction proofs. Since no letterpress image comes between original type design and the film negative, the image exposed to the printing plate is not liable to any of the imperfections that may occur in letterpress printing. The letter images will be as perfect as the original drawings of the letters themselves.

Besides providing a cleaner, sharper image for the camera, photocomposition has other advantages. For one thing, it often saves time since one entire step—making the reproduction proof—is eliminated. It also permits greater variety and flexibility in the choice of type sizes, in the fitting together of the letters and words, and in the positioning of the lines because of the versatility and the focusing facility of the camera lens. These things, of course, are rigidly fixed in metal typesetting.

The New York Times
Large Type Weekly

Regular spacing

The New York Times
Large Type Weekly

Tight spacing

Sometimes photocomposition can lower costs, since the camera supplies the platemaker with composition and final film all in one step—and all made up and ready to go. Savings are particularly likely in advertising work where letters and pictures can be brought together in one film assembly, eliminating studio charges for the making of a "mechanical"—that is, mounting, in the proper position on a single board, the units of type proofs, lettering, photographs, and drawings for the camera.

Photocomposition can also be economical for the production of large units of "straight" body copy where many lines of the same length of the same type and the same size follow one after the other. This is particularly true if the photo-typesetter is controlled by a computer. When such a combination is used, great speed—far beyond Gutenberg's wildest dreams—can be attained. The Bible, which took that inventive gent five years to complete, has been set by a computer in seventy-seven minutes! However, it should be pointed out that the programming may have required three to six months. As the years go by and programs become more sophisticated—and programmers more efficient—this time for "feeding" the machine is becoming shorter and shorter.

Finally, because offset printing and photographic typesetting are both two-dimensional, they make a more sympathetic and logical team than three-dimensional typesetting and two-dimensional printing.

At the present stage in the development of photocomposition there are still, to be sure, some problems. In particular, existing letter styles must be redesigned if the original character of such time-honored and proven types as Caslon and Baskerville and Garamond and Bodoni are to be retained.

When a letterpress proof is made from metal type, the impression left on the paper is significantly different from the actual face of the type. Ink tends to spread and cover a bit of the sides, as well as the face, of the type. As the type is pressed into the paper, the strokes that make up the letter—straight *and* curved, thick *and* thin—soften to some degree, while sharp angles and corners become rounded. It is the appearance of this *printed* letter that the original designer envisioned and that we admire, not the sharp image of the drawing itself.

Enlargement from 10 point film type

Enlargement from 10 point metal type

The camera, then, is a demanding master. Photographs of the original letter image not only eliminate the imperfections that sometimes occur in letterpress printing; they are, in a sense, too perfect. All the strokes appear to be too fragile; sharpness is emphasized, and the beauty and legibility that made the type great—as *type*—are distorted, if not actually destroyed, in a photographic facsimile of a letter image originally conceived for reproduction from metal type.

To insure the survival of our historical types while we enjoy the new speed and efficiency of photocomposition, tomorow's designers will need to study and interpret them in the light of the camera's super accuracy. This is already being done to some extent. The task is not an easy one, even for those who have been trained in the customs of fine printing, and it will be virtually impossible for many of today's younger designers and artists, who have had comparatively little exposure to this tradition. Nevertheless, a look back over the long history of the twenty-six letters convinces us that successful adaptations *will* be made. Other obstacles have been overcome and only a true pessimist would believe that this one won't be, too.

Just as important—perhaps more so in the years ahead —will be the need for *new* designs and *new* techniques especially directed toward new methods of typesetting and printing.

In this period of experiment and confusion, most fine type houses recommend a combination of both metal and film for greatest efficiency and best results. There are some areas in which film setting can easily do a job which would be next to impossible with the old method, and some areas in which setting metal type is still the best. The industry is developing new techniques and new abilities with such startling ingenuity, however, that this situation could change overnight.

Several kinds of machines are now being used to produce photographic composition. They differ in the techniques they employ, but in principle they are similar.

A sort of drum, or grid, contains all the letters of a particular alphabet family—capitals and small letters, roman and italic, numerals, punctuation marks, and all the other characters that make up the family. This complete "showing" is scanned in proper sequence and position by flashing stroboscopic lamps, and it is projected onto photographically sensitive film.

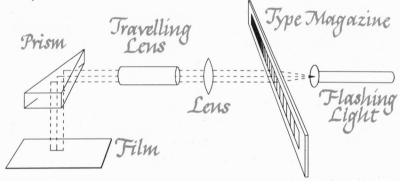

The lens makes possible an almost infinite number of variations. One master alphabet can be projected in a great variety of sizes and weights and angles of slant, with spacing and positioning from very tight, where the letters may even touch or overlap, to very open, where large spaces show between the characters. Lines can be curved and distorted and moved about with the greatest freedom.

When the film is developed, only the images of the exposed letters, placed according to the original plan or layout, are recorded.

That is the simple principle of phototypography.

Photocomposing machines, as we have mentioned, are capable of greater speeds than traditional hot-metal devices. An experienced Linotype operator can set and cast about five characters a second and a tape-operated casting machine can produce only seven to ten. Photocomposing machines, on the other hand, are physically capable of exposing up to five hundred characters a second. In practice, however, the speed of the manually operated photocomposing machines is limited to the skill of the keyboard operator. Even when more than one keyboard is used at the same time, it is still impossible to take full advantage of the machine's potential rate.

The breakthrough came in early 1963, when the printing trade announced that digital computers were being successfully experimented with for operating photocomposition machines.

Digital computers are really calculating machines. They differ from regular nonelectronic devices in their ability to process letters and other signs and symbols as well as numbers. They can also compare different bits of information and they can store and recall this information after it has been fed, or programmed, into them. They can produce the results of their computations in a readable form —and their work is done at fantastic speeds.

The reason for this speed is that digital computers process information in the form of electrical impulses—and the speed of electricity is practically instantaneous. Some computers are capable of producing a billion pulses per second!

Programs can be submitted to the computer in any of three forms: punched cards, punched tape, or magnetic

tape. In each case, the information to be processed is converted into yes-no, on-off—that is, pulse–no-pulse—form;
either the electrical charge is active, or it isn't. Most computer composition today is done with punched tape, so we
will consider only that form here. The principle for all
three is, of course, the same.

TAPE LEVEL	VALUE OF HOLE
6	32
5	16
4	8
3	4
2	2
1	1

33 7 12 20 11 31

TAPE LEVELS							CHARACTERS AND FUNCTIONS	
6	5	4	FEED	3	2	1	Unshift	Shift
	●	●	•				a	A
	●		•		●	●	b	B
		●	•	●	●		c	C
	●		•		●		d	D
	●		•				e	E
	●		•	●	●		f	F
		●	•		●	●	g	G
			•	●		●	h	H
	●		•	●				
			•		●	●	1	⅛
●	●	●	•			●	2	¼
●	●		•				3	⅜
●		●	•		●		4	½
●			•			●	5	⅝
●	●		•	●		●	6	¾
●	●	●	•	●			7	⅞
		●	•	●				

For every hole in the tape, as it moves along, an electrical pulse is generated. The position of the holes across the width of the tape determines the action of the pulses. The holes are so arranged that they can give the computer all the instructions necessary to produce the wanted results. The end product is a magnetic tape that is especially adapted for operating the composing machine—that is, for "instructing" the composing machine what characters to expose to the film and in what sizes, weights, and positions.

When a film typesetter is operated by a computer, instructions are stored in the computer's memory; then the operator selects what he wants simply by pressing the correct keys. The programs also store special rules and commands that execute practically all of the functions of the old-time hot-metal compositor.

Besides the actual setting of type, the computer can perform many editing jobs, such as compiling indexes, bibliographies, footnotes, and the like. Special items can be picked out of the body of the manuscript as the composition progresses, stored in the memory, sorted, recalled, and then set according to the prearranged program.

One must remember that both the Linotype operator and the computer programmer work with their hands, and production is limited to human abilities. However, once the tapes for either method of composition have been punched, the great speed of the computer in performing all the various instructions makes the real difference in the time consumed in the preparation of copy for reproduction.

Impressive as the computerized photocomposing machine is, it is not the latest of the new methods for typesetting now being considered by commercial users of the alphabet.

In recent years entirely new devices for producing print-

ing copy have been introduced—devices that can compose
up to ten thousand characters a second by entirely electronic means, thus doing away with photocomposing
machines. Perhaps this is the direction in which commercial typesetting is headed. However, the great expense
of the new equipment may prevent many printers from
adopting it quickly, despite the lower labor costs that
would result. Right now it is too soon to tell.

Electronic typesetting systems literally "paint" letters
and other characters on the face of a cathode-ray tube (a
flat disk coated with aluminum and phosphor)—similar
in many ways to the making of a television picture. These
images are projected on film which is used for processing
the sensitized plates. The letters are produced on the face
of the cathode-ray tube by the swinging in short parallel
strokes of an electronic beam. These beams are so fine

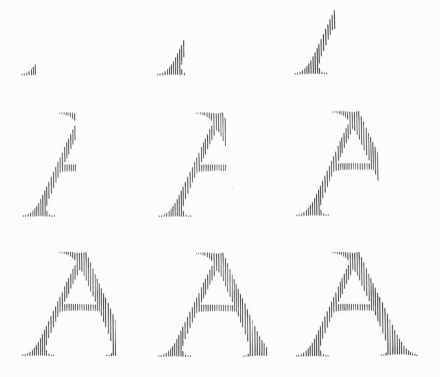

(something less than a thousandth of an inch) and the strokes are so close to each other that the resulting image appears to be solid. Some machines produce horizontal, others vertical, strokes.

The beam is switched on for a very short time and its length is no greater than the size of the letter being made. Since as many as ten thousand letters per second are possible, you can see that they are "painted" at a very great rate indeed, in preselected order and prearranged patterns.

After the electronic beam has created the letters on the face of the tube, the result is projected onto the film for the printing plate. This is done in several ways. Some machines, using either stationary or moving lenses, transfer the characters to moving film as they are produced. Other machines paint a complete page before it is projected on film. Still others compose a line at a time and this is projected, as it is completed, onto a film which is so controlled that it advances a predetermined distance after each line has been recorded.

For fine typography—work that can compare in beauty and effectiveness with traditional methods—the cathode-ray-tube principle may not be the final answer. No matter how fine those beams may be and how close together they may be placed, a curve must still be made up of a series of straight lines!

Now, however—almost in recent months in fact—an answer to this problem may be in the works. Entirely new electronic experiments are being made which may overcome the shortcomings of cathode-ray-tube "painting."

The new technique employs the laser (an acronym for Light Amplification by Stimulated Emission of Radiation). The laser produces a very thin, very intense beam of light that can be controlled with great accuracy to create letters that are more faithful to the original than those produced by cathode-ray-tube painting.

With this astonishing beam, the recording of letters is no longer limited to straight strokes, but the light can be so controlled that it will follow any pattern, any curve, any variation in width and length and direction with hitherto unknown intensity and accuracy. It can be made to record the most intricate designs. Its ability to reproduce shapes with complete fidelity to the original pattern, as compared to cathode-ray-tube painting, may be seen in the following simulation.

Let us say we want to reproduce this calligraphic *a* . . .

The cathode-ray tube will re-create the form with extremely thin, tightly packed strokes like this . . .

Now the laser beam can be so controlled that there are no longer any gaps or approximations in the final result. The laser recording light can be directed in any pattern and at any preselected spot in the design. Its limits may be compared to the almost infinite number of possible curves in a fine French curve, used for generations by draughtsmen to produce sharp, precise shapes which are too intricate and too time-consuming for construction with compass and rule.

The laser beam can, say, move this way . . .

and this way . . .

The upper closing stroke is made with . . .

and we have produced this much of the letter . . .

Next we reproduce the right-hand stem . . .

and finally, the finishing serif . . .

We have now made without any short parallel straight lines a near-perfect picture of the written letter, so nearly a facsimile of the pen-drawn form that not even the calligrapher who wrote it could find much to criticize.

It should be emphasized, however, that this is an infant development and its future is unknown. As with all new things, its value will be as great or as small as the taste and knowledge and technical skill of those who pursue it. As we write these words, this astounding example of modern science appears now to be something that future letter artists and typographers and printers, as well as the great world of readers, may well be affected by. Perhaps it is the discovery we need to bring together those who long for the continuation of our traditional letters and those who must concern themselves with economical, competitive, high-speed, no-nonsense printing.

There is always a danger of becoming so entranced with speed and efficiency that we may forget that suitability to use is still the most important element of any typographic job. Naturally, different uses demand different approaches. A printed list of the players in a high school basketball game, for instance, has a one-time, short-lived purpose and it would be foolish to spend a lot of money to make it a lasting work of art. On the other hand, we should avoid *any* production methods that detract from the beauty and quality of work that is meant to last.

It is clear that the future of the twenty-six letters is becoming more and more dependent upon technicians. This could, of course, spell the end of beauty in favor of economy and efficiency. There really is no reason, however, why the designer and the technician cannot work together to maintain our typographic traditions and produce printing efficiently. If the technician is given some background in design and the designer some knowledge of the limitations and possibilities of the machine, there is hope that this alphabet of ours can survive the "efficiency" and continue to be beautiful, useful—"congenial," to use Hermann Zapf's term—as well as utilitarian.

We have watched the alphabet evolve from a prehistoric painting on the wall of a Spanish cave—discovered by a girl and brought to the attention of the world when she called to her father, "Toros! Toros!"—to the most intricate, most complicated, almost other-world developments of electronic letter-making.

The fabulous new machines we have been talking about will either preserve for your future use the alphabet of the past in an efficient, modern, thoughtful way or, if you let them, make it as out-of-date as the handsome hieroglyphics became when other then-modern commercial scripts were introduced to serve more efficiently business and literature.

It is unlikely that your author will add another chapter to this story twenty years hence—but others will, you may be sure. The almost unbelievably complicated things that are happening to the making of letters today will most surely seem in 1990 as simple and primitive as Herr Gutenberg's contribution seems to us today.

Dominus vobiscum. Alpha-beta!

DICTIONARY INDEX